From Cod to Callaloo

The story of Bristol through Food and Wine

For Louisa and Joe

From Cod to Callaloo

The story of Bristol through Food and Wine

Sue Shephard

 redcliffe

First published in 2013 by Redcliffe Press Ltd
81g Pembroke Road, Bristol BS8 3EA
www.redcliffepress.co.uk
e: info@redcliffepress.co.uk

ISBN 978-1-908326-43-0
British Library Cataloguing-in-Publication Data
A catalogue record for this book is available from the British Library

Cover image: courtesy Bristol Museum's Natural Science Collection

Cover design and typesetting by Stephen Morris www.stephen-morris.co.uk
Original photography by Stephen Morris
Set in Garamond 12pt/14
Printed by Zenith Media Tonypandy

CONTENTS

Acknowledgements

I am very grateful to all the librarians, archivists and historians whose help is so important when researching a book of this kind. In particular, I would like to thank the librarians at the City of Bristol Central Reference Library and the University of Bristol Library – especially Michael Richardson in Special Collections. I am also grateful to the Bristol Record Office, the Somerset Heritage Centre, the Bristol Branch of the Historical Association and the Bristol & Avon Family History Society. Staff at Bristol Museums, Galleries and Archives, including M Shed, Blaise Castle Museum and the Bristol Museum and Art Gallery, have been most helpful and generous with pictures for the book – in particular Catherine Littlejohns, Julia Carver, Jenny Gaschke and Rhian Rowson. Many thanks to Tristan Pollard at the Royal West of England Academy for help with Ellen Sharples' recipe book. My thanks too to the Frenchay Village Museum.

I would like to thank the following people for advice and help: Evan Jones, Eugene Byrne, David Eveleigh, the late Mick Aston, James Russell, Paul Townsend, Ian Haddress, Madge Dresser, Toby Musgrave, Barney Haughton, Fiona Beckett, Laura Mason, Tom Jaine and Laura Rowe.

My special appreciation and gratitude must go to food historian Peter Beard for kindly allowing me to reproduce his drawings and for invaluable help. To my historian husband Ben Shephard for his unfailing support, to my editor Ann Kay, publisher John Sansom, and wonderful designer Stephen Morris. Also to my dear friend Tim Mowl for constant encouragement, enthusiasm and hand-holding.

Sue Shephard, Bristol, September 2013

Introduction

THE KITCHENS *of* HISTORY

Food is not simply the staff of life – it is the stuff of history

One day, I was eating in one of Bristol's Jamaican restaurants and was served a traditional dish of codfish with callaloo. As I sat admiring the colours and enjoying the lovely aromas, I began to think about how far the ingredients for this dish had come – not just across thousands of sea miles but through several centuries of Bristol's history.

It has been a long journey from the Icelandic dried cod that Bristolians ate during the early Middle Ages to a Caribbean spinach called callaloo. This is a story unique to Bristol – of ships and trade, wealth and hunger, maritime exploration and slavery, and includes many kinds of food and drink, such as wines and sherries, sugar and spices, chocolate and self-raising flour, bananas and charity buns.

One would expect a proper history of a great city like Bristol to include kings and queens, wars and politics, religion and, in Bristol's case, slavery, and readers might reasonably ask, what has food to do with history and what can it tell us about the lives of Bristol's citizens? For a long time historians were rather snooty about including food in history. Then, in 1832, the Scottish historian Thomas Carlyle struck a note of revolt against solid history books. 'The thing I want to see', he wrote, 'is not Red-book lists and Court Calendars and Parliamentary Registers, but the Life of Man in England: what men did, thought, suffered, enjoyed', and as he referred to the 'passions of the stomach' he no doubt meant to include what men (and women) ate as well. A century later another historian, Sir Harold Acton, took the argument a little further: 'The great historian now takes his meals in the kitchen', he wrote. Nowadays food historians use all kinds of clues about what people ate and how they cooked to explore the past.

The story of Bristol and its connections with food is, of course, a great deal more than what went on in the kitchen and on the dinner table. As well as cooking, eating and drinking there is the city's trading life and its links with the sea and the world beyond. Indeed, food and drink are so closely bound up with Bristol's history, and have played such an important part in the city's trade, politics, religion and social life, that the picture would be incomplete without them. Bristol's very character and purpose was founded on trade, including cod, wines, spices and sugar. While for its merchants, food was a source of profit, for its citizens, food was a marker of status: white or black bread, fresh or salt fish, meat or no meat, a well-stocked spice cupboard or a handful of herbs, plentiful supplies of precious sugar or a little honey – all spelled wealth or poverty and having the means to survive or not.

Long before a Bristol merchant ship was towed up the tortuous bends of the Avon and slipped through the towering gorge into the safety of the city docks, food was already a vital part of the economy of south-west England. Iron-Age people guarded their homes and hunting grounds here and later the Romans used the Bristol region to produce food supplies for their armed forces. From the Middle Ages on, Bristol's merchants played a part in England's colonial history; their ambitions to find better trade routes, fresh markets and bigger profits opened wider worlds of new lands and new foods. But the huge wealth gained from trading in slaves has left an indelible stain on Bristol's past.

This book is an attempt to look at the story of Bristol through food and drink by exploring the daily lives of its people; the power of the merchant class; the extraordinary maritime voyages; the changing place of women in the home; the observations of its visitors; the inventiveness of its business-men; and the culinary legacies of waves of invaders and settlers that made it the rich and diverse city it is today. It is not, of course, the whole story. There are inevitably numerous important Bristol stories and people, events and places that are not included here. I have attempted to offer a flavour and a picture to show how, in diverse and sometimes unique ways, food and drink have shaped the character and fortunes of this special city.

THE IRON AGE
'Industrious and Fairly Civilised'

Imagine a young Iron-Age warrior standing guard on a promontory of the cliff that rears up above the Avon gorge. He can see his fellow lookout posted atop the vertical rock on the opposite side of the river. Or he can look to his right, across a deep-cut wooded gulley where a third man guards the river Avon as it makes a slow, wide curve around a marshy plain which, in some 500 years, will form the Saxon site for the town of Bristol.

People still come to this viewpoint in Leigh Woods and pause to admire the extraordinary view. Standing here they can look down at the sluggish river below or across to the cliffs soaring up to Clifton village, the flat green playground of Durdham Down to the left and, to the right, Brunel's suspension bridge, which seems to float at eye level. Only the roar of traffic thundering along the Portway below spoils the sense that one is looking into the past through centuries of change to the very beginning of Bristol's history. If you turn your back on this view you can clearly see among the trees the impressive mounds and ditches of an Iron-Age hillfort – the dramatic evidence of people who, centuries before a bridge was erected or a stone wall raised, built fortified camps above the river to guard their homes. They were the first Bristolians.

Since Prehistoric times, scattered populations of Neolithic and Bronze-Age tribespeople had lived and hunted in the Bristol region, leaving their evidence in burial tombs, sarson stones and tumuli. By the late Iron Age, however, the area was occupied by just one tribe, the Dobunni. The Dobunni built hillforts with massive earth ramparts topped with stone to guard access from the sea to their tribal lands, which stretched from Cirencester in the north to Glastonbury in the south. The young warriors were kept on constant watch for aggressors from Europe, Ireland and Wales. Unlike the large, fair-headed Belgic Celts who dominated most of England at this time, the Dobunni were small, dark people who had arrived from Iberia around the first century BC. They settled in the Somerset Levels, where they lived in stockaded villages built on stilts in shallow lakes. But when they found that they

'Gorge of the Avon with Iron-Age tribespeople.'
An imaginative drawing from *Bristol: Past & Present* by J.F. Nicholls & John Taylor, 1881

were vulnerable to attack and flooding, many moved on to safer places such as the caves in the Mendip hills, the heights of Clifton Down and the Avon gorge, or onto fertile lowlands and marshes around the Avon river basin, where they were well protected by their hillforts.

Thanks to Arthur Bulleid, a Victorian archaeologist, who found extensive remains of a lake village near Glastonbury, a great deal is known about the Dobunni people. They were not, as he explained, 'the woad-daubed Savages of the Old History Books', but were 'industrious and fairly civilised'. Bulleid's discoveries give a vivid picture of how they lived, what they made and how they produced, cooked and ate their food.

The Dobunni were expert spinners, weavers, carpenters and potters. They mined iron ore from the Mendips which they smelted to make sharp-edged tools and weapons and cooking equipment. Cooking was revolutionised as soon as the Dobunni were able to hammer out iron pots or cauldrons. These could be hung, or stood directly, over the flames of the fire and would not break or crack through over-heating. More hygienic than earthenware pots, iron containers could be cleaned out with sand, ash or water.

Food remains show that the Dobunni were resourceful hunters and farmers. Their diet was varied and exploited anything edible that lived or grew

A reconstruction of a Dobunni family preparing a meal. Note the rotary hand quern used to grind the grain, the iron cooking pot by the fire, meat hung up to smoke in the smoke hole and a recently killed swan brought in to be plucked and roasted. Although chickens were known to have been introduced into Britain in the middle of the first century BC, they were still a rarity and it is unlikely that they would have been pecking for grain in the floor of this hut. Drawing by Sir Armédée Forrestier, 1911. Courtesy of the Somerset Heritage Centre

around them. Archaeologists described finding 'wheelbarrow loads' of grains, pulses and sloe stones, a large variety of wild berries and the remains of leaves, seeds and fruits of at least 40 edible plants. In winter they hunted in the forest for deer, elk and wild ox. They killed otter, beaver, fox, boar, weasel, pine marten, polecat and hedgehog. Remains of a great variety of waterfowl were found, including cranes, swans and even pelicans. In summer they fished in rivers and lakes for a huge variety of fresh and saltwater fish, shellfish and even frogs.

They cleared woodland for fields where they pastured sheep, goats and pigs, used oxen for tilling the fields and horses to pull wagons. They ate mutton and drank milk from goats, ewes and cows. Milk stored in pottery containers quickly soured, producing curds and whey, and so cheese and butter-making soon evolved. Cultivated crops of spelt, rye and wheat barley were harvested with iron hand sickles. The Dobunni knew how to prevent cereals from sprouting and rotting by parching (burning handfuls of stalks of grain and beating off the grain as the husk burnt), but some unparched seed was kept for sowing the following year. They used various types of quern to grind the cereal into a rough flour, which they made into hearth cakes or unleavened bread to be cooked on hot stones on the edge of the fire. Fragments of a kind of 'bread' were found which consisted of unbroken wheat grains moistened a little with honey or fat to make an unbaked loaf which would have been extremely hard to eat and digest and very damaging to the teeth. It is probable that it was soaked in broth or milk to soften it before eating.

The warm, wet climate made it difficult to preserve food for winter. Without the help of salt, which was then very scarce, the Dobunni were nevertheless able to wind-dry and smoke some of their food, especially a glut of fish or meat. They knew how to dry and store surplus cereals, peas, beans, nuts and berries in pots high off the ground or in deep sealed pits, while many edible plants and herbs were dried and stored on racks. Their religion focussed on the natural world around them, with plenty of feasting and drinking. Fermented honey was made into mead and later beer was brewed from barley or wheat. Cooking was determined by the availability of fuel, cooking pots and weather. Meat and fish were either skewered on green sticks and barbecued on the open fire or broiled on hot stones, or stewed in wooden or leather containers. Some unplucked birds were smothered in thick clay and baked in the embers and large eggs were buried in ash. One very early form of cooking, still popular in homes without a fireproof pot, was pot-boiling: a pot, or pit lined with stones or wood to make it waterproof, was filled with water. Meanwhile, stones were put in the fire until they were really hot and were then placed in the water so that it slowly reached boiling point. Vegetables and possibly a piece of meat or fish were put into the simmering water. As stones cooled, freshly heated ones replaced them.

The Dobunni tribespeople who lived in the Bristol region were productive and mostly peace-loving. Life on the whole remained stable and prosperous despite sporadic raiding parties, disease (malaria was rife in the Somerset Levels), poor harvests and hungry winters. They traded their pots, woven cloth and metalwork as far as the Mediterranean – where perhaps they heard of the impending Roman invasion of Britain which would change their way of life forever.

ROMANS IN BRISTOL

Portus Abona

Just after the little train that runs between Bristol Temple Meads and Avon-mouth has shot out, with a triumphant hoot, from its tunnel under the Downs, it makes a stop at Sea Mills station. This small, insignificant-looking settlement on the flat mudbanks of the Avon is all that is left of a Roman port called *Portus Abona*. People think they can see Roman remains of a harbour wall and a bridge, but these are, in fact, an eighteenth-century attempt to create a tidal harbour, which was built on top of Roman ruins. A Roman road once ran from here through today's northern suburbs of Bristol, across the Downs and on to Bath, but there is no evidence of it now. Modern Sea Mills gives no sense of the bustle and drama of the little Roman port, and it requires all the imagination one can summon up to see what was once here, or to hear the hammering, clanking and shouting, the swish of ropes and slap of oars. It is hard to see how this rather bleak riverbank, strewn with tidal rubbish and covered over with housing and allotments, could ever have been the economic and military hub of the south-west, or to imagine it as the vital commercial forerunner to the great maritime trading city of Bristol that would appear seven miles upriver several centuries later.

The Roman conquest of Britain in AD 43 was a well-coordinated effort by land and sea and the Bristol Channel would have been busy with Roman troopships struggling to make headway up its treacherous tidal waters. Shore parties were landed to establish lookout points and bases from which to find vital supplies of foodstuffs and horse forage for land forces that were moving slowly but methodically from the east to the west of the country.

Although most of the Dobunni people signed treaties of friendship with their new masters and adopted a Romano-British lifestyle, the hostile, fierce tribes in Wales refused to submit to Roman rule and were a serious threat to the Roman military camps established on the Welsh side. Even in the vast barracks at Caerleon on the river Usk, housing up to 6,000 men, it was found

A Roman tombstone found at Sea Mills. Possibly Christian, third century BC, and thought to have been erected to the wife or daughter of Caius Sentius

to be difficult to produce supplies of food, equipment and luxuries, which instead had to be produced and delivered from occupied Britain. For this, a supply port was needed, and the Romans found the perfect site for a small, secure base less than a mile from the mouth of the Avon, where it is joined by its tributary the Trym. (At this time the Bristol Channel was considerably wider and the river Avon shorter and deeper.) They named it *Portus Abona*, meaning a naval base on the river Avon. Here they quickly constructed a fortified port and a walled naval garrison with a lookout tower to keep watch on the river approaches. Its docks offered unique facilities for re-manning, re-victualling, storage and ship repair, with wharves and quays, timber yards, chandleries, smithies, ropewalks, sail lofts, granaries and warehouses. There was at least one large villa, barracks for soldiers and several cobbled streets with workers' houses and a bridge across the lower reaches of the river Trym. There was also a small temple with a carved stone altar bearing the motif of an eagle surmounting a globe with a cornucopia – a symbol of abundance and nourishment advertising the Romans' capacity to procure food wherever they went, which is just what they intended to do in the Bristol region.

By the time the Roman invasion had been successfully completed, the Dobunni territories in the Bristol region had become part of a vast Imperial agricultural estate whose function was to supply the Roman forts in Wales with food and equipment. Safely tucked up in the mouth of the Avon, *Portus Abona* became the principal port shipping supplies to the Welsh garrisons. It was also used as a ferry station for troops and for the passage of officer-class Romans to agreeable shore leave at Bath. The crews of coastal patrols operating swift, double-banked liburnae were also stationed there and Roman gold was brought through *Abona* to pay troops and civil servants. From here the Roman administration took control of the region and turned *Portus Abona* into a small but flourishing military and civilian town.

The intelligent Dobunni took the opportunity to trade their wares and skills with military and civil administrators and were also converted to Christianity, when it reached Britain in the late second century. Increasingly, the Romano-British came to profit from the benefits and pleasures of life under Roman rule, especially the food. One thing that traders and local people began to notice with some astonishment was how much the Romans loved their food. Plain old Celtic stews, roasts and hard bread were of no interest. Rather like the currently fashionable Mediterranean diet, the Roman diet was very healthy. They cooked with wine rather than milk and with olive oil instead of butter, ate plenty of fish and were very enthusiastic about pulses, vegetables and salads.

Romans also poured richly thickened or piquant dressings over their dishes and loved pungent, intense-tasting flavours, pepping up their food with sour pickles, sweet preserves, spices, aromatic marinades or fermented sauces. The most popular of these was a fermented fish sauce called *garum* or *liquamen*, which was often used in place of salt. It was copied from the Greeks, who had been producing a fish sauce for centuries. The Roman version used small red mullet, sprats, anchovies or mackerel, which they mixed with the entrails of larger fish. This was then salted and put in a vessel to rot in the sun. After a while the concentrated juice was removed with a sieve and stored in earthenware amphorae. Liquamen was produced around the Mediterranean on a vast commercial scale and sent all over the Roman Empire. Every soldier had his own small, stoppered jar of the pungent sauce, which he sprinkled liberally over his food. The most novel characteristic of Roman cookery was the complexity, variety and amount of different flavours and ingredients – many

WHAT THE ROMANS BROUGHT WITH THEM

The Romans were probably the first people to have the idea of enclosing large pieces of land as game parks where they kept and hunted red, roe and fallow deer, wild boar and even bear. Newly introduced game birds such as peacock, pheasant and guinea fowl were also kept in enclosures. They introduced the Spanish rabbit and brown hare and created enclosures called *leporia* where they were bred and fattened for the table. Contrary to popular legend, dormice were rarely eaten except at banquets. For these they were kept enclosed in pottery vessels and fed on acorns and chestnuts until they were fat enough. They were then stuffed with minced pork and dormouse meat and baked in the oven.

Snails were a common delicacy that was especially popular in the Bristol region. The Romans introduced a kind of large edible snail that had to be kept on land entirely surrounded by water to prevent it escaping. They were fed on milk, wine must, spelt and wheat. For the final fattening up, when the snails became so fat that they could not get back into their shells, they were put in jars with air holes. They would then be fried in oil and served with fermented fish sauce mixed with wine. Like the ever-popular oyster, snail shells have been found in huge quantities on many Romano-British villa sites. In Somerset there is a very long tradition of rearing and eating these snails, locally named 'wall-fish'. It is said that descendants of Roman snails are still being fattened and eaten today.

The Romans loved all kinds of fish: freshwater fish were often kept in fishponds, including eel, perch, pike and carp – and also frogs. They especially liked shellfish such as crabs, lobsters and oysters, which were transported live in water tanks to markets. It is thought that oysters were successfully farmed around the mouth of the Avon. Sea fish were caught from offshore fishing boats with line and hook. Cod, haddock, herring, sea bream and grey mullet were popular – even blubber from an occasional stranded whale.

The Romans used large amounts of honey in their cooking. Bee-keeping increased substantially and new varieties of honey arrived from southern Europe. Cheese-making also

increased, particularly soft curd cheeses from the Mediterranean that were used in patina dishes or mixed with meat or fish, hard-boiled eggs, nuts and seasonings.

The Roman capacity for drinking wine was enormous and, although viticulture was possible in southern Britain (evidence of vineyards has been found in the Bristol region, where the climate was drier and warmer at that time), vast numbers of wooden barrels or amphorae of wine were imported from the Mediterranean region and south-west France.

Some Vegetables and Salads Brought in for Cultivation

Cabbage, beets, turnips, globe artichoke, marrow, asparagus, broad beans, cardoons, peas, leeks, kale, garden carrots, parsnips and onions. Lettuce, endive, cucumber, celery, mallow, arache, corn salad and fat hen.

Cultivated Orchard Fruits and Nut-bearing Trees

Lemons, walnuts, almonds, medlars, sweet chestnuts, apricots, mulberries, damsons, plums, figs, table and wine grapes, sweet cherries and new varieties of apples and pears.

Herbs and Plants Used for Medicine and Cooking

Garlic, parsley, chervil, fennel, dill, garden mint, thyme, rosemary, rue, shallot, bay, basil, hyssop, rocket, sage, savory, sweet marjoram, radish, anise, oregano, borage, asafoetida.

New Cereals

More productive varieties of cereals including a new type of wheat called spelt, which grew well in the British climate. It could be sown twice a year, increasing productivity significantly.

Game

Pheasant, peacock, guinea fowl, fallow deer, Spanish rabbit and brown hare.

Luxury Foods Imported from the Roman Empire

Olives and olive oil, *liquamen* sauce, wine and vinegar, caraway, sesame, celery and poppy seeds, dried fruits such as raisins, apricots, sultanas, figs, dates, pine cones and kernels. Also honey from southern regions and various kinds of preserved hams, sausages and pickled fish from the Mediterranean. Varieties of dried beans, lentils and chickpeas.

SPICES

For use in medicines and to enliven dishes the Romans imported a vast range of expensive spices from around the world including pepper, cinnamon, ginger and cumin.

A wealthy Roman's spice cupboard contained a formidable list of dried herbs and spices – pepper being the most highly valued.

of them highly exotic and unusual – in a single dish. Romans wanted food that tasted exciting, looked attractive and showed off both their wealth and their cooks' skills in the kitchen.

Increasing quantities of the Romans' favourite foodstuffs arrived at *Portus Abona* on ships loaded with amphorae of olive oil and wine, jars of sauces and vinegar, seeds of fruits and vegetables, new breeds of fat livestock and exotic-looking fowl and game. The wharves would have been stacked with sacks of grain and dried beans, casks of butter, mountains of big cheeses, sides of pork, mutton, venison and beef, baskets of vegetables, fruits and herbs, and bundles of dried, salted fish. Every day stevedores would load cargo ships as they waited for the tide to carry them downriver, into the Channel and up the coast of Wales to feed thousands of hungry Romans. Soldiers on the move carried their own basic food allowance and foraged or stole what they could. But when based in camp their diet was more varied and provisions were sent in from the surrounding farms set up under Roman supervision.

The Romans brought their own farming practices and made British farm workers adapt to their methods of ploughing, sowing, manuring and harvesting crops, feeding cattle with turnips and rape, and growing winter fodder. Instead of allowing domestic animals to roam in the countryside, they kept them in enclosed fields or stalls. Bread was still the staple diet and local grain supplies had to be hugely increased to meet demand. Large granaries were built with raised floors and ventilation slits and also kilns for drying and parching the grain before threshing. At Caerleon, for example, a lead bread stamp reading 'Century of Quintinius Aquila' was found, which suggests that each century of soldiers (100 men) baked their own specially labelled bread in large beehive bread ovens. The soldiers consumed quantities of salt pork or mutton, fried or stewed in a porridge of cereals and herbs. Officers, of course, ate better and could enjoy boiled chicken, roast boar and venison bought ready-cooked from the bath-house vendors. At Vindolanda, in the north, the commanding officer sent his slave a shopping list of things to purchase for his table:

> bruised beans, two modii, twenty chickens, a hundred apples, if you can find nice ones, a hundred or two hundred eggs, if they are for sale there at a fair price … 8 sextarii of fish sauce … a modius of olives …

By AD 75, a large civilian Roman town called Venta Silurium was established in Wales directly opposite the mouth of the Avon, and regular ferries crossed from *Portus Abona* to service its needs. Gradually, the region was given over to profitable civilian enterprise, with small farms, villas and workshops. By the second century, Abona had become less military and its role as a small market town substantially increased. Traders, with their own ships, workshops and stores, established themselves there, building houses and settling their families. It became an import and export centre supplying not only victuals for soldiers, but better class things for the villas, farm estates and towns in the region. British beer, glassware, woollen clothing, woven flax for togas, decorative ware for villas such as mosaics, furniture, pottery bowls, storage jars, cooking pots and pewter kitchen- and tableware all came in and went out on ships from *Portus Abona*. Goods were taken on the new fast roads which connected the port with Gloucester to the north and Bath and London to the east. But food remained the main business in the Bristol region; Gatcombe and Wraxall were grain producers and the salt pans of Banwell were used to salt beef, a major staple foodstuff of the army.

Although the south-west was not highly populated during the Roman occupation of Britain, there were several villas and farming estates, such as those at Aust, Ashton Park, Wraxall, Lye Hole, Blaise, King's Weston, Wick, Bedminster, Butcombe, Keynsham and Somerdale, and at the Bristol site itself there is thought to have been at least one villa on the north bank of the river Frome (located at what is now Upper Maudlin Street). Between Bristol and Keynsham, beneath a busy main road and a Victorian cemetery at Durley Hill, lie the little-known remains of one particularly substantial villa, which some archaeologists believe is one of the grandest and most opulent of its type yet discovered in Britain. The unusual scale and layout of the 'Keynsham' villa indicates a splendid building erected for someone of considerable wealth and importance – probably a Roman senator or retired military officer of high rank. Dozens of rooms, with underfloor hypocaust central heating, were connected by a colonnaded veranda built around three sides of a courtyard with ornamental gardens and gravel pathways. The most exciting discovery at this villa was of two unusual hexagonal structures jutting out from two corners of the building, each of which contained a dining room called a *triclinium*, so-called because it had three recesses with three couches for reclining diners. The walls were decorated with painted plaster and the floors with splendid mosaics featuring birds, foliage and scenes depicting classical myths such as Europa and the bull. Probably one *triclinium* was for family dining, whilst the other was kept for formal banquets.

The legendary Roman orgies of saturnalia, with feasting, drinking, visits to the vomitorium and erotic entertainments, were rarely found in Roman Britain. Even the temptations of the resort of *Aquae Sulis* (Bath) nearby, with its medicinal thermal baths, sacred springs and other diversions, did not offer much of a decadent lifestyle. But a religious holiday or other special day of celebration would have been an opportunity for the occupants at the Keynsham villa to move into the grander triclinium, invite some guests over and order sumptuous and inventive dishes from the kitchen. Tables were elegantly laid with knives, spoons, ladles, cups and finger bowls, made of pewter, silver and glass. Forks were not known for eating with until the seventeenth century, but a small, double-ended spoon called a *cocleare* was used – the bowl end for eating soft food and sauces and the pointed handle end for picking shellfish out of their shells and possibly for picking one's teeth as well. Slaves removed guests' shoes and replaced them with sandals, hands were washed in special bowls and a fine white napkin knotted around their necks. After saying prayers, the feast could begin.

But by the end of the fourth century, the stable, comfortable life enjoyed under the Romans was coming to an end. Britain faced increasing attacks from barbarians – Picts, Scots, Welsh and Irish. Several Roman legions were withdrawn to defend Gaul, which was being threatened by Germanic Saxons, leaving the country vulnerable and undefended. Romano-British leaders appealed to Rome for help but were abandoned and left to their fate. The year AD 410 spelled the end of over three-and-a-half centuries of Roman occupation. A new, quite different and powerful force now began to take over the country and turn Romano-Britons into Anglo-Saxons.

THE ANGLO-SAXONS
Bread, *Briw* and Ale

After nearly 400 years of relative peace and security under Roman rule, the British people were ill-prepared to defend themselves. Even before the Saxons arrived, the Picts and Irish had begun to plague the vulnerable Bristol region and much of the population fled from the towns and farms to seek shelter in the old Dobunni hillforts. The humbler Romano-British establishments – small villas, farms, rural settlements and industrial sites – continued as before, though they were often plundered for their food or products. Irish barbarian raids of AD 367 partially destroyed the King's Weston and Blaise villas. Archaeologists found burnt roofing and human bones in the debris of the Keynsham villa, where several skeletons were discovered in the well. As the defunct villas crumbled around them, the more enterprising took building stone and roof slates to erect their own simple shacks or shelters. Gradually they took over the ruins, where several families might now occupy one room and cook on an open hearth in the once-sophisticated kitchen. Cooking reverted to old Celtic routines of stews, flat bread, foraging for fruit and nuts and, occasionally, a piece of roast game meat. Almost everything the Romans had brought with them disappeared, rabbits and game birds went feral and a few plants seeded themselves in the countryside but most died out.

The Saxons reshaped the British countryside with their villages, farmsteads, field systems, fisheries and woodland. Within a century or so the British had abandoned their own Celtic tongue and Romano-British place names were changed to Saxon ones. The Saxons brought new methods of farming, different people as slaves and their own Germanic traditions of food and cooking.

There were several monasteries, royal palaces and manors in the Bristol region, including an important one at Cheddar. The country people living in the area were the tenants and were expected to take their grain to the manorial mill for grinding and pay a toll with a proportion of their grain. Similarly, they were supposed to take their dough to be baked in the bread oven and leave some loaves in payment. Not surprisingly, many quietly continued to use hand querns to grind their flour and bake unleavened hearthcakes at home. The poor were forbidden to kill and eat wild animals that roamed the parks and woodland or to fish in the weirs and fishponds stocked with eels and fish – all of which were the property of the manor. Meat or fish was therefore rarely found in the cottage cauldron. But everyone ate bread, whether it was refined or coarse, leavened or raised.

As in so much of medieval life, the quality of the food people ate depended upon status. Bread in particular was graded from heavy, dark bread to the finest white. The modern words 'lord' and 'lady' come from the Old English *hlaford*, meaning 'the keeper of the bread' or 'breadwinner', and *hlafdig*, meaning 'the maker' or 'the kneader of the bread' (*hlafaeta* were the bread eaters). Wheat was used to make soft white breads for the rich, which included sweet cakes spiced with cumin, caraway, poppy and sweet cicily seeds and dried, honeyed fruits. The commonest peasant bread, called *maslin*, was made from a dough mixture of wheat, barley and rye flour, while some country people discovered that small raised loaves could be cooked in a makeshift oven formed by inverting a deep pot over their dough to make it rise.

Another Anglo-Saxon daily staple was stew (*briw*) or broth consisting of seasonal vegetables (called 'potherbs'), cereal or pulses and occasionally a little chopped meat or fish, slowly stewed together in a pottery or iron cauldron over the open fire. Most peasants made do with a thin briw or a thick pease pudding. The commonest vegetable stews used roots, cabbage, leeks, onions and wild garlic. Cereals and pulses might be added to thicken the mix. Small pieces of salt bacon, along with pork fat and some bone marrow, provided the usual small amount of protein to go into the stewpot that stood over the more fortunate cottager's fire. Almost all cooking was done in a simple, three-legged cauldron, since this was the most efficient use of firewood and did not waste precious cooking juices. It meant that a stew could be left to simmer slowly over the fire for several days. Anything that came to hand could be put into the stewpot, from bits of meat or fish to cereals, seeds, the leaves and roots of wild plants such as the small wild carrot, parsnip or turnip plus onion, field garlic, leeks and mint to give more flavour. It all got cooked up slowly into a rich broth. The addition of cereals, seeds and pulses thickened the mixture – as they cooked, the grains burst open and released their starch into the broth, causing it to thicken into a satisfying purée or porridge. The stew was kept simmering day after day with bits and pieces added as and when they became available. Although it sounds quite nutritious, the vitamins were mostly boiled away and scurvy was endemic among the poor.

The Anglo-Saxons were great ale drinkers as water was avoided because it was usually contaminated. Traditionally, women did much of the brewing and they knew how to produce yeast for both baking and brewing. Ale houses became a feature of every village and wayside tavern. Bee-keeping was another important activity as honey was the only sweetener. It was also the major ingredient in producing mead – a sweet, heady alcoholic drink of fermented honey first developed by the Celts. Cider and perry from apples and pears were also popular.

Powerful Saxon kings began to carve up the country and introduce a very different style of administration and rule. By the seventh century the west of England was divided into two regions, with the river Avon as the boundary between Mercia to the north, ruled by Anglian kings, and Wessex to the south, under West Saxon kings. Life was far from safe or peaceful. Barbarians from the west and north continued to harass the country but a far greater and more dangerous foe were the ferocious Vikings, who came in their fast, silent longships across the sea from Daneland.

On Twelfth Night in AD 878, a Viking army made a surprise raid on the town of Chippenham, where the Saxon king, Alfred of Wessex, and his court were wintering. Caught unprepared, Alfred was forced to flee. According to popular legend he disguised himself as a herdsman and reached the 'fen-fastness' of the Somerset Levels near Glastonbury, where he sought sanctuary in a shepherd's hut. The shepherd's wife told the disguised king to sit by the fire and keep watch on her cakes cooking on the hearth while she went out to feed the chickens. But Alfred was so concerned by the predicament of his country and people that he fell into a deep reverie and forgot the cakes. When the woman returned she found her cakes were burned. She berated the herdsman and turned him out of her home.

King Alfred certainly did have to escape a surprise Viking attack in Chippenham and he did flee to Athelney near Glastonbury, where he raised a new force and successfully beat back the Viking army threatening his kingdom. But it is the legend of the burned cakes that has endured over the centuries. Perhaps it made the king seem human and fallible but also out of touch with the everyday business of life, which for much of the population revolved around the basic need to find shelter and food. These cakes were not anything like the modern concept of a cake, but were made with a coarse dough, patted into hearthcakes or flatbreads and baked on the hot stones beside the fire. People in the Bristol region were known to have baked various kinds of barley bread and oatcakes called *havercakes* or *clapbread*. But when the harvest was poor, a really rough bread was made using flour ground from dried beans, pease, buckwheat, acorns, hazel and alder seeds and, in particularly

A woodcut illustrating a seventeenth-century ballad about Alfred. From *The Roxburghe Ballads*, vol. III, 1880

lean times, even weed seeds and tree bark. If Alfred had indeed burned the cakes, it could have been a disaster for the shepherd's wife, whose family may have gone hungry that day.

King Alfred spent much of his rule forging alliances with other Saxon kingdoms, fighting the Vikings across Britain and preventing Viking attempts to conquer Wessex. In order to protect important places from Viking attack and to control the surrounding region, Alfred ordered the building of fortified towns called *burhs* to act as both a trading point and military stronghold. Although Bristol is not recorded in King Alfred's *Burh Hidage*, it is thought most likely that the town was first laid out as a *burh* sometime in the late ninth or early tenth century by either Alfred's son Edward the Elder (then king of England) or his son-in-law, Aethelred of Mercia. After her husband's death, Alfred's daughter, Aethelfred, completed the programme of fortified towns; so a woman might well have been responsible for the creation of Bristol.

No one really knows exactly when Bristol was founded, or who transformed

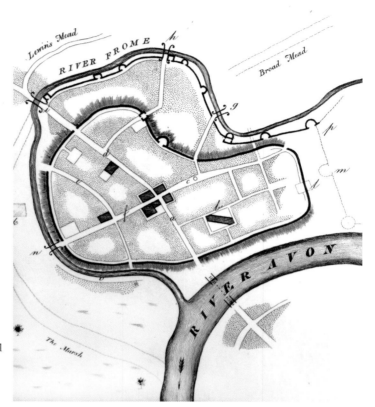

Detail of a map by Samuel Seyer (c. 1821) showing the Saxon layout of the *burh* of Bristol. Courtesy Bristol City Library

it into a fortified town and why. But there seems little doubt that, for some time, there had been the need for a ford between Mercia and Wessex at a convenient and safe point on the Avon. A site near the convergence of the rivers Frome and Avon would seem to have been an obvious one. Gradually, the site's value as a border and as a river crossing for travellers and traders meant a settlement of some kind with a market place had begun to appear. The earliest name, *Brycg stowe*, meaning 'the meeting place by the bridge', suggests that a small settlement of traders and rivermen were already living around a bridge at this point. But if Bristol really began life as a *burh* it would not have evolved slowly from this small settlement by a bridge but was more likely to have been quickly built and fortified to the classic Saxon plan.

The new town was set on a raised promontory encircled on three sides by water. Flowing along the south was the tidal river Avon while its tributary, the river Frome, curled around the north and west. Together they formed a protective skirt of water. A stronger wooden bridge replaced the original simple

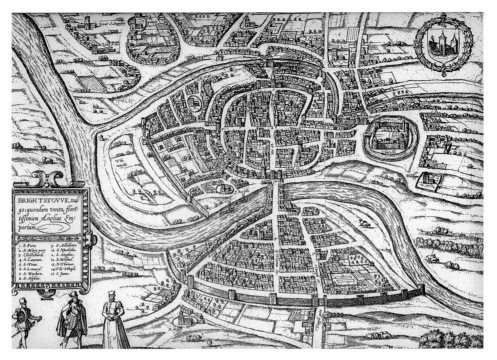

Ricart's *Plan of Bristol* (1591) from the *Maire of Bristowe is Kalendar*, is the earliest known town-plan in Britain. Although later than the Saxon *burh*, it does show the original street layout with the High Cross at the centre, and the Norman castle and moat. Courtesy Bristol City Reference Library

structure across the Avon and a smaller bridge crossed the Frome to the north. Four main streets were laid out and named Corn Street, Broad Street, High Street and Wine Street, with small lanes of houses and gardens crammed in between. One long street ran around the entire inner defence wall. *Brycg stowe* became *Brigstowe* and quickly blossomed into a thriving market town, a river port and possibly even a Minster, with two churches, St Peter and St Mary le Port.

At first, householders in the town had good-sized gardens in which to grow potherbs and keep bees, chickens and a pig. Some also held land outside the town where they pastured livestock or grew their cereal crop. Already, a large amount of dried cod known as stockfish was being imported from Icelandic fish traders to supplement the shortage of meat. The lack of winter fodder in the countryside meant that most livestock were slaughtered in the autumn and preserved for eating in winter time; only breeding and draught animals were kept over winter. The family pig could provide enough fat and pork to feed a household until the following spring. Nothing was wasted, from snout to tail: the heart would be cooked, salted and hung up to dry; the cheek pieces went into the brine crock to cure; the belly would be salted and used for soups and stews; the bones could be preserved in brine for stocks and flavouring; and the fat was preserved for frying and roasting. The most valued cuts of bacon and ham were carefully salted, dried or smoked and hung high up in the chimney away from insects and bacteria. With all this preserving and pickling, salt was in huge demand. Such a valuable product attracted a hefty salt tax and, as it was one of the most expensive food products in the household, it was kept locked in the spice cupboard. Only the best-quality meat would have been salted; hence the expression 'not worth its salt'. The animal parts that could not be preserved were put aside for a great cook-up by family members and neighbours. Offal, tripe, heart, ears, feet and cheeks were made into brawn, fried chitterling and blood sausage. This feasting on fresh meat helped to fatten everyone up and see them through the lean winter months ahead.

Like the old Roman *Portus Abona*, Bristol's earliest identity was soon established as a fortified, maritime port; a place that was well guarded and safely tucked out of the sight and reach of marauding pirates and enemy ships. Merchants built timber wharves along the riverbanks and brought increasingly large ships upriver laden with goods from abroad, which were then sent on along the old Roman roads to Bath, London and the north. To maximise profits, merchants built their own ships and manned them locally. Shipowners gradually increased their fleets and exported regional woven cloth, leather hides, fine flax linen, British beer (which was popular on the Continent) and silver and iron ore from the Mendip mines. In 1009/10 a coin of King Aethelred was issued from Brigstowe, which proves that by then it was an important market town with its own mint and trading port. Although this period as a late Anglo-Saxon fortified *burh* was short-lived, it was most likely here that the ancient foundations of Bristol's maritime character and merchant greatness were laid.

THE MIDDLE AGES
Normans, Nobles and Merchants

BRISTOU CASTLE – THE RICH MAN IN HIS CASTLE

Walking around the city centre today it is hard to see anything very ancient about Bristol. Great slabs of graffiti-covered concrete are slammed up against what remains of the medieval town, and only a handful of churches and the original street layout offer clues to its origins. But if you turn your back on Broadmead shopping centre and the lost river Frome flowing somewhere below the car-choked streets, you might wander into a forgotten warren of scoops and mounds around the blitzed remains of the church of St Peter and find occasional bits of wall and the deep, empty cut of a castle moat. This is more or less all we have left of the castle built by strange foreigners, known as Normans, who took over and, once again, transformed the country's culture, buildings and cooking.

In 1066 William of Normandy invaded and was crowned King of England. Two years later he marched west to enforce the submission of the towns of Exeter and Bristol. He appointed his close friend and secretary Geoffrey de Coutances as Governor of Bristol and gave orders that the town be strongly fortified with thick stone walls and, on the unprotected east side, a castle was to be built in the proper Norman way with a great earth mound topped with high wooden stockades.

Saxon noblemen were evicted and their manors seized by Normans. Yet much of the complex Saxon hierarchical order remained (the Normans called it 'feudal'), and more regulations, dues and taxes were introduced. In 1086, in order to extract the maximum in taxes, King William ordered a survey to be made of England, which came to be known as the Domesday Book. Bristol at this time formed part of the royal manor of Barton and the only reference to the town in Domesday is that *Bristou*, the new Norman-French name, paid dues of 110 marks of silver to the king and 33 marks to Geoffrey de Coutances – a relatively large sum for a small town. Although Bristol hardly merited a mention in Domesday, whilst much of the country was struggling with Norman oppression, the town was booming and was already an important port with access to the main sea routes. With its strategic position, strong fortifications and burgeoning maritime trading, the town was rapidly growing in size and importance. The new link with Normandy in France opened further trade and galvanised the town's economy.

Bristol merchants have always been prepared to trade in anything that was profitable, from leather, wine and dried fish to slaves. The place was already a major centre for the slave trade – an association that would continue to dog the city over the centuries and from which it grew wealthy. Romans and Anglo-Saxons had been enthusiastic slavers, and for generations Bristol's merchants had been shipping men, women and children, captured in Wales or northern England, to Dublin, where Viking barons controlling the region sold them on throughout the world. For a while the Church tolerated the trade, though it banned the sale of slaves into 'heathen' lands. Wulfston of Worcester, the last Saxon bishop under the Normans, whose diocese included Bristol, was appalled by the sight of slaves in Bristol and regularly preached against the trade:

> They used to buy men all over England and carry them to Ireland in the hope of gain; nay they even set forth for sale women whom they had themselves gotten with child. You might well groan to see the long rows of young men and maidens whose beauty and youth move the pity of a savage, bound together with cords, and brought to market to be sold.

Eventually, King William clamped down on the trade 'whereby heretofore men used in England to be sold like brute beasts', and in 1102 it was banned. But Norse-Irish traders were loath to give up their lucrative source of slaves and even decades later there were stories of them inviting unsuspecting people aboard their ships in Bristol, whereupon they would suddenly up anchor and sail off to Ireland.

After the death of King William in 1087, Geoffrey de Coutances used Bristol as his headquarters in a rebellion against William's son, William Rufus, a very unpopular king who was eventually murdered whilst hunting. When William Rufus' brother Henry I took the throne (1100), Bristol and its castle continued to play a vital role in the many royal conflicts that followed. De Coutances died in 1093 and the castle was handed to Robert FitzHamon, who had vast estates in England, Wales and Normandy. In 1121 FitzHamon's daughter Mabel was given in marriage to Henry I's favourite illegitimate son Robert of Caen, who was subsequently made Earl of Gloucester. Bristol castle became the couple's principal residence. Robert, a cultured and learned man and a keen patron of new religious orders, founded St James' Priory in Bristol. He was also a great builder and turned his attentions to the castle.

Robert rebuilt the castle in stone brought specially from Caen, France. (It is said that he ordered every tenth stone to be laid aside for the erection of St James' Priory.) There were dungeons, a moat on the east side joining the rivers Trym and Avon, a drawbridge with a great stone keep, a massive tower crowned with four turrets, a chapel, stables, workshops, private apartments, separate kitchens and a fine banqueting hall with massive timber roof. A contemporary description at this time pictures the castle 'rising on a vast mound strengthened by wall and battlements, towers and divers engines', straddling the eastern, landward end of the peninsula, 'with two rivers washing its sides and uniting in one broad stream lower down where the land ends', so that this natural moat 'hems in the entire circuit of the city so closely that the whole of it seems either swimming in the water or standing on the banks'.

Bristol castle became one of the strongest and most impressive in the country. The Earl and Countess of Gloucester lived here in considerable comfort and style, presiding over a large and busy household which included clerks, guards, kitchen and household servants and the cook. (The master cook was, around this time, a particularly valued and well-paid member of the household; William Canynges the Younger [1399-1474], a hugely wealthy merchant, shipowner and four times mayor of Bristol, would later have a tombstone dedicated to his cook laid near his own in St Mary Redcliffe church.) With a constant round of visiting royals, churchmen and noblemen expecting lavish hospitality and entertainments, one can picture in Bristol castle the life of a Norman nobleman and his household.

While ordinary working people made do with coarse barley bread, salt pork and beans and were not expected to know about etiquette, the upper classes dined on fresh meat seasoned with expensive, exotic spices and displayed refined table manners. Like the Romans, from whom they took inspiration, the Normans had a passion for a kind of food that was well outside the ordinary man's idea of a daily meal on the table. For them, a dish should be transformed by taste, texture and appearance into a culinary work of art which, through the combination of skilled cooks and luxury ingredients, displayed the wealth and good taste of the diners. But it was not simply ostentation that dictated their diet. The Normans, like the Romans, were obsessed with complicated fears concerning eating and health. Many foods were considered dangerous to the bodily 'humours' unless they were correctly balanced with others. Cabbage, which was considered warm and dry and bad for the digestion, could be neutralised with oil, marrowbone or egg yolks; cucumbers,

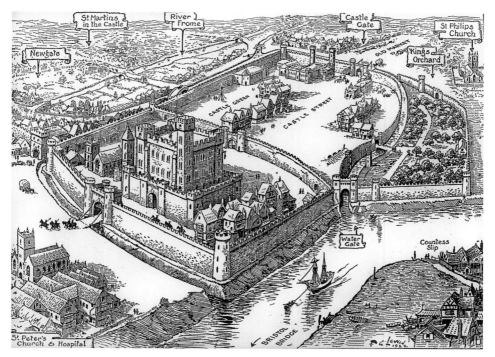

Bristol castle as envisioned by FG Lewin, 1922. Courtesy Bristol Reference Library

thought to be cold and humid, were prepared with honey and oil; raw fruit was dangerously cold and should be cooked in warming wine and spices; lampreys were so dangerous that they had to be drowned in red wine or salt before being roasted with warming herbs and spices.

The kitchen in Bristol castle would have been large, well equipped and staffed with experienced French cooks, assisted by dozens of under cooks and apprentice boys who lived in the kitchen and slept on the floors (there were no female cooks). As a fire precaution, the kitchen was built of stone and sited separately from the main building. There would have been an impressive array of pots and pans, spits and cauldrons, mixing bowls and jugs, cleavers, knives and mallets, tongs for cutting sugar, bunches of twigs for whisking sauces and pestles and mortars for grinding spices – a great *batterie de cuisine* kept to hand for the cooks as they worked around a huge table, chopping, slicing, mincing or pounding meat, fish and vegetables. Meanwhile, washing boys, bent over tubs of scouring sand, were kept busy with the washing up.

Most of the cooking was done at a great fireplace where large joints, even whole oxen, were roasted on spits held on giant firedogs. Spit boys basted the meat with long basting ladles whilst trying to protect their faces from the

Medieval cooks and cook-
boys doing various tasks in
the kitchens. Drawing by
Peter Brears from the
Luttrell Psalter (c.1340)

searing heat. Iron cauldrons, hung over the hearth on pot hangers, bubbled
with elaborate pottages. Like the Saxon *briw*, some form of pottage was a
staple in every household, high or low. The Normans introduced several versions of what they called *pottage* or *porray*, such as a thick pottage called *runnyng*
and an even thicker one, which could be sliced, called *stondyng*. One popular
thick cereal pottage was *frumentie* or *furmenty*, made of boiled, hulled wheat
and milk of almonds and rather like a creamy porridge but to which meat
such as venison with saffron and other spices could be added. A more
luxurious pottage called *mortrew* was also made – with ground beef and pork
boiled in wine and served in a wine sauce that was thickened with capon
meat, almonds and breadcrumbs, seasoned with cloves, sugar and fried almonds and coloured with indigo or a red dye.

The bakehouse was also a separate building to protect against fire, with
ovens built out from the walls. A good fire of wood, peat or furze heated the

oven until it was hot enough, then the embers were cleaned out with long-handled rakes and the loaves of bread, pies, tarts and enriched breads and pastries were set in the oven using flat hardwood peels or shovels. Baked pies, or *bakemetes*, were particularly popular. Because medieval pastry rarely contained fat and was hard as rock, the pastry – or *coffyn* – was not eaten. The crust wall of a large pie had to be strong and solid as it was intended to act as a container in which to bake the contents, which could then be scooped out and eaten. A pork pie, for example, was painted with saffron and egg yolk and baked to a deep gold; when cut open, the meat filling was revealed, patterned with gleaming black prunes and bright discs of hardboiled eggs, rather like the pork pies of today. *Minst Pyes* were originally filled with various spiced meats chopped fine; later, dried fruits and sugar were added and the beautifully decorated pies became traditionally eaten in midwinter and around Christmas and known as 'Christmas Pye'. It was not until the nineteenth century that the meat ingredient was dropped and mince pies became wholly fruit-filled.

The master cook and castle steward together held responsibility for the preparation and serving of dinner at noon. The first thing they had to consider when planning the daily menu was what day it was – a meat day or a *Fysshe* day? The Church ruled that in each week there were two fast days – Friday and Saturday – when only fish was permitted and eating meat in any form was forbidden. There were also longer, stricter fasts, such as six weeks during Lent when neither meat, dairy products nor even eggs were allowed. Unless the lord was wealthy enough to own his own fishponds, or lived near large rivers or the coast, the supply of fresh fish was very limited and most had to make do with salted or dried fish. Fortunately, the kitchen in Bristol castle would have been amply supplied with freshwater and sea fish as well as coastal shellfish. There are records of monasteries with fish ponds, or 'stews', in Somerset producing huge amounts of fresh fish for the Bristol market such as bream, pike, roach or trout, while fisheries on the Severn yielded thousands of eels, which could be eaten either fresh or salted. Because of their 'fish-like' tails, some marine or semi-aquatic animals – such as whales, barnacle geese, puffins, or even beavers – were declared 'not meat' and could be eaten on fish days. Nobles, unable to eat meat on fast days, could still be sure of dining in style. Dinners held on fish days were splendid affairs and popular for serving illusionistic or 'mock' food that imitated the forbidden meat, cheese and eggs in various ingenious ways. Fish could be moulded to look like venison or replaced meat in the form of imitation hams and bacon; almond milk replaced animal milk as an expensive non-dairy alternative; *Eyroun in Lentyn* were faux eggs made from sweetened almond milk cooked in blown-out eggshells, flavoured and coloured with spices. Designed to fool

A cook with flesh hook. The large flesh hook was used to remove pieces of meat. A similar one was discovered during an archaeological dig on the site of a Norman house in Tower Street, Bristol

the eye and palate on fast days, these dishes also provided amusement by turning the ordinary into magic.

The French cook in charge of the kitchen at Bristol castle, with his large army of specialist bakers, sauce-makers and confectioners, no doubt knew what was most favoured and suitable for his master and family. They enjoyed strong flavours, showy-looking dishes, lots of colour and plenty of variety. Their favourite tastes were spicy or sweet-sour, including the tang of ginger, the subtleties of cinnamon, the heat of pepper or mustard and the sweetness of honey tempered with vinegar. They particularly liked thickened sauces and custards. Nothing was appreciated more than a colourful sauce or spicy stuffing that could turn plain meat and fish into something festive. A white chicken stew might taste delicious but looked insipid, so one cook decided that it needed a touch of colour: 'When you serve it forth, powder thereon a spice that is light red coriander and set pomegranate seeds with comfits and fried almonds round the edge of each bowl.' Black sauces, made from blood and offal, might accompany a roast swan or pheasant, while the deep, rich yellow of saffron was used in custards and *frumenty*. One popular green sauce for fish used parsley, sage, mint, costmary and dittany, thickened with bread-crumbs and tempered with vinegar or ale. White dishes were thickened and coloured with ground almonds, almond cream and sugar.

The master cook kept an armoury of expensive ingredients, colourings and spices, including sugar and salt, locked in his spice cupboard. He got supplies of fresh herbs, fruit and vegetables from the castle gardens and or-chards, milk, butter and cheese from the castle dairy, wines and ales from the cellars and daily deliveries of fresh meat and fish. He would have made sure he was among the first to hear of a ship newly arrived with a cargo of

A cook in his kitchen. Note the cauldron hung on a ratchet so it can be raised or lowered over the fire. From Nicholls & Taylor, 1881

almonds, spices, wines and dried fruits. Almonds were the most popular luxury ingredients and featured in numerous dishes. Huge quantities were needed for thickening, flavouring and colouring. Almond milk was used extensively in a whole range of dishes, from savoury puddings to sauces for meat or fish. It was made from ground almonds steeped in either water, wine, ale or fish broth to make a 'milk' with a consistency which varied from 'thryfty', or thin, to 'good and styfe'. Almond cream, a thicker version of the milk, was a useful alternative to dairy products and eggs during Lent when their use was forbidden. Wine, vinegar and verjuice were cook's most trusted standbys. Verjuice was made from unripe green grapes (or crab apples); its very sharp, tart, mouth-puckering taste was much loved, especially when tempered with the sweetness of honey to create a sweet-sour flavour. Favourite

A Taste For The Exotic

In the twelfth century, during the early Crusades, new spices and strange, exotic dried fruits from the East began to appear in England. Sugar was still very rare and the alternative sweetness from 'raisins of Corinth' (currants), figs and dates was especially appreciated. Dried fruits and new varieties of spices were used in festive pottages and pies during Christmas or Lent, when merchants could be sure of big sales. One Bristol merchant, who had commissioned a load of figs and raisins from southern Spain to sell at Easter, refused to accept delivery of the cargo because the ship was badly delayed by storms and did not reach Bristol until well after the end of Lent. The first Englishmen to enjoy oranges and lemons were probably the Crusaders wintering with their king, Richard I, in the fruit groves around Jaffa in 1191–2. Citrus fruits, which originally came from northern India, remained relatively unknown in England, and it would be many years before they routinely appeared on any but the wealthiest nobleman's table.

dishes had surprising flavours such as tansy – a popular choice at Easter. For example, tansy leaves were pounded in a mortar and the juice added to beaten egg, which was then made into an omelette with a tart, distinctive taste.

When at home, Robert, Earl of Gloucester, and his family dined every day with the household in the great hall of the castle, and everyone was expected to attend. It was always a formal, public occasion at which the earl could reaffirm his authority and status. He could also be approached after the meal, when he might hear requests and complaints or hand out a rebuke or favour. The earl was particularly strict about only French being spoken in the castle as he claimed that 'unless a man knows French, people think little of him'. At one end of the dining hall was a raised dais on which the lord, his family and visitors were seated, facing out on one side of a long trestle table. Several other tables were ranged around the hall where members of the household and lesser visitors were similarly seated facing the high table. Cleanliness and good table manners were important and washing before a meal was essential. Women were so concerned to appear refined that some would eat beforehand and merely toy with a morsel at the dinner table in order to keep their elegant fingers and fine clothes unsullied with food. The earl and his wife had eight children who, when they were old enough, ate in the great hall with their nurse. They were carefully instructed in good table manners, using books written for the upper classes. Rules for refined behaviour included: no belching, spitting, putting your fingers in the food, picking your teeth, blowing your nose on your napkin, swiping your neighbour's food, licking out a dish, scratching for fleas or whispering among friends. Everyone had their own

A twelfth-century fish-day meal. The man in the centre holds a knife and trencher. The page offers a beaker of wine which will be shared by the guests.
Peter Brears

napkin, spoon and knife but shared from dishes of food and cups of wine. Instead of plates, diners ate off thick slices of stale bread called trenchers which had a slight hollow in the centre to hold the sauces and pottage broth. It must have been tempting to eat your trencher, richly soaked in delicious flavours, but this was not encouraged as the trenchers and leftovers were gathered up at the end of the meal and later given to the poor.

Because salt was considered the most essential and expensive condiment, the lord would have had an extravagant and showy silver salt cellar centre-stage at his table. This practice of advertising wealth must have impressed two Bristol merchants, William Bird and Thomas Bath, who were recorded as possessing valuable silver salt cellars. Dishes were served at table in 'messes' of two or four portions, to be shared by the diners at table. The best dishes were sent to the top table whilst the tables of the household's lower ranks were offered inferior choices. The earl and his family ate freshly baked white bread made with fine wheat flour but his staff and less important guests were given plainer white bread and at the bottom end of the hall the labouring staff ate brown rye bread and pottage. When the meal was finished, the tables were cleared and the workers went back to their duties. If the earl had guests, they retired to a separate chamber and were served spiced sweet wine called *hippocras* (also *hipocras* and *hypocras*) with wafers and sweetmeats. Finally, after grace had been said, the earl rose to drink a toast as a signal that dinner was over.

Bristol castle would always remain in royal hands, separate from the town itself. Kings and queens came and went using it as an occasional refuge or resting place, a base from which to raise funds or forces and imprison their rivals and enemies. After Henry I died in 1135, his daughter Matilda claimed the throne. But her cousin Stephen seized it instead and quickly moved to reduce the power of Matilda's half-brother and ally Robert, Earl of Gloucester. He laid siege to Bristol castle, which, thanks to Robert's building works, proved impregnable. After defeat at the battle of Lincoln, King Stephen was brought to Bristol and locked up in the castle. Later, however, the tables were briefly turned when Robert himself was captured by the king's supporters, exchanged for Stephen, and imprisoned for a while in his own castle. Matilda, meanwhile, had brought her 9-year-old son, Henry of Anjou, to Bristol, where he could be 'instructed in letters and trained up in civil behaviour'. But after Robert of Gloucester died in his castle in 1147 and was buried in St James' Priory, Matilda abandoned her claim to the throne, made peace with Stephen and returned with her son to Normandy.

In 1154, the 21-year-old Henry returned and was crowned England's first Plantagenet king. He did not forget his time as a child in Bristol castle and retained an affection for it, spending lavishly on improvements: he added a barbican before the main west gate, a gate tower and a magnificent great hall. Within a year he had also granted the town a charter:

> Know ye that I have granted to my burgesses of Bristou that they shall be quit of toll and passage and all custom throughout my land of England, Normandy and Wales, wheresoever they and their goods shall come.

King Henry also handed Dublin to Bristol to colonise and, after he had conquered south-east Wales, further opened trade with Wales. Considerable numbers of Irish and Welsh migrants settled in Bristol, one or two of whom later became prominent merchants and officials.

In 1347, Edward III granted Bristol further liberties and powers and later, in 1373 after the town had contributed several ships to the king's naval fleet fighting in the French campaign, he made it the first English town outside London to be granted county status and Bristol's first sheriff was appointed. To mark this, a City Cross was erected at the top of High Street.

BRISTOU TOWN – SHIPSHAPE AND BRISTOL FASHION

With the benefits of royal favours and charters, Bristol trade took off. Its earliest prosperity was at first built on trade with Ireland. With a brisk traffic in corn, hides, wool, salt meat and dried fish, carried up and down the river Avon, dozens of ships crowded the wharves, waiting to be loaded and unloaded. Then, in 1152, Henry II married Eleanor of Aquitaine and the rich vineyards of Gascony came under English rule. This presented a golden opportunity for the merchants of Bristol and they quickly exploited this new market. The city's ships were soon importing thousands of tuns of wine a year, mainly from Bordeaux. In those days cheap wine was more commonly drunk than either beer or water, which was mostly filthy and undrinkable. Vast quantities of Gascon wine, a pale, light red claret which did not keep well, were stored in the city vaults and in the castle cellars. Bristol now had a safe port, ample cellarage, carrier routes to take goods to the main cities and fleets of barges or trows to take wine inland via the Severn or over to Wales. With the great West-Country wool-producing regions around Bristol, and the increasing domination of Bordeaux among the wine-producing regions of south-west France, wool and wine became the great staples of overseas trade. Bristol's importance as a port became second only to London.

But increasing sea trade was causing serious problems with the numbers and size of ships attempting to come upriver and berth in the city docks. The huge tidal range of the Avon had always caused difficulties. As the water in the river ebbed back towards the sea, ships anchored in the harbour became stranded on the riverbed and suffered immense pressure from the weight onboard, which often caused considerable damage to the timbers. As a result, Bristol-built ships were specially constructed with rounded hulls that could rest safely on the mud. Sailors visiting the port would comment on this, spawning the famous saying 'shipshape and Bristol fashion'. Bristol burgesses were faced with the challenge of huge and expensive improvements if the town was to keep pace. A 'Great Ditch' was constructed in St Augustine's Marsh to straighten out the course of the river Frome and provide more space for berthing ships. Although Bristol was built so far inland, it always had the air of a seaport. With ships coming right into the heart of the city, their tall masts and high prows dominated the scene. The smell of the sea and the noise of cranes and shouting mariners gave an unmistakable marine character.

Bristol was now full of merchants' houses, warehouses, craftsmen's shops and homes with their gabled roofs leaning to meet one another across dirty, dark and confined streets. The town's growing population was squeezed inside its high perimeter walls. The town gatehouses, each with a church, kept watch on everyone coming and going and were closed for the night curfew. The

Church was the focus of the community and there was an explosion of church building and the founding of monasteries and hospitals. St Augustine's Abbey, later to become the city Cathedral, was consecrated c. 1146 and some grand civic buildings such as the Guildhall went up in the town centre, with the first mayor of Bristol elected to office in 1216. Wealthy merchants, shipowners, prosperous officials, lawyers and physicians built themselves grand mansions of stone or brick along new wide streets; a few even had glazed windows and tall chimneys. Ships could sail into the heart of the town and unload their cargos on the quays beneath the merchants' windows. This was predominantly a male world but there were a few exceptions of women working as independent traders. Alice Chestre was the widow of a Bristol draper who had carried on with his successful trading ventures at a time when Bristol's cloth exports had trebled. After her husband's death, Alice continued his business trading in cloth, wine and food commodities with Ireland, Spain, Portugal and Flanders, often in her own ships. She was also responsible for having a crane built for loading and unloading ships. She was unusual in this respect, as most merchant widows seemed to have traded just long enough to honour their late husband's outstanding contracts before retiring to comfortable widowhood. Alice was rich enough to build herself a grand house with living quarters over her ground-floor shop off the High Street. At this time, there were terraces of shopkeepers' houses in the market area (around St Mary le Port) that had their shop fronts open to the street. Land prices were high and, in the cramped conditions of the medieval town, many people, including Alice, had to live above their work.

For the majority of ordinary Bristolians, medieval town life was noisy, dirty, stinking and difficult. The poor were crammed into tall, timber-built thatched tenements that were often sub-divided into small rented rooms where whole families struggled to survive. Children grew up playing in the dark, narrow, cobbled streets, which were little more than open sewers. Some houses had a backyard or alley where there might be a small oven built into the wall or sometimes an open hearth over which they could hang a cauldron of pottage to simmer all day with whatever could be afforded from the market or foraged from the countryside outside town. Few had access to a kitchen, or even a hearth, and many did not own equipment even for basic cooking. Buying from food vendors was their only option. There were such people everywhere, in the streets, down on the wharves or in the market place; jostling crowds, rowdy taverns, shouting street vendors hawking their wares and trays of food: 'hot peascods' (whole young peas, boiled and then dipped in butter and vinegar), 'hot sheep's feet' or 'ribs of beef and many a pie'. Swelling the numbers of town residents was a daily influx of itinerant

Cooking in a medieval town-house. The better-off could afford to eat well, with more variety.
Peter Brears

craftsmen, traders and travellers of all sorts such as monks, beggars, clerks, pilgrims, preachers, messengers and even a knight on horseback or a retinue of carriages with a nobleman and his family travelling from one estate to another. Foreign merchants and ships' captains off their boats from France, Spain and Portugal stood around the docks chatting in their own language while the sailors got drunk in dockside ale houses. On market day the place was full to bursting with peasants with heavily laden mules, farmers' wives bringing in eggs, herbs and vegetables, traders' carts loaded with kegs of butter and huge Cheddar cheeses and drovers arriving from the Midlands and Wales with sheep, cattle, geese or goats. They took their animals to the shambles – the slaughterhouse or butcher's row – on the riverbank, where they would be slaughtered before the butchers shouldered the still-dripping carcasses back to their shops to be cut up into joints.

For people living in the countryside, things had not changed very much; they continued with the daily grind of producing their own food and coping with bad weather, poor harvests and outbreaks of disease. But for those who had moved into the towns to find work, living conditions and the business of eating was dramatically different. Life in town still centred on finding food but now, instead of growing it themselves as they had once done in the country, these new townspeople had to buy it and of course earn the money to pay for it.

Town dwellers with money certainly ate better than their country cousins. They had more choice of food from the market stalls, food shops and even places where they could buy ready-cooked meals. They could nip to the bakery, butcher or fishmonger's stall or send out a servant to the cheesemonger, pie baker, saucerer or waferer for a ready-cooked dish or pie. The numerous daily visitors and travellers, not wishing to carry provisions with them, relied on takeaway food services. Though still restricted mostly to seasonal fare, customers were able to buy fresh each day. Many could now eat white bread instead of coarse rye bread and buy cuts of fresh lamb or beef as well as seasonal herbs, fruit and vegetables. If they were wealthy, like Alice Chestre, they could also buy luxury foods such as sugar, wine, almonds, dates, spices and exotic fruits such as lemons, oranges and pomegranates. Even the frugal housewife could visit the spicerer to buy cheaper mixed spices in bags of powder *forte* (strong) or powder *douce* (mild). She could also buy little packets in more affordable quantities of unrefined brown loaf sugar (sugar sold in a large block) and packets of salt. One of the great enduring myths about food in the past is that spices were used to preserve or mask the flavour of rotting meat or fish. This is nonsense; spices were far too expensive to be wasted on bad meat, and similarly salt was only used to preserve the best cuts of meat and fish – although for long sea voyages poor-quality flesh was steeped in vats of cheap brines and vinegars, with the pickle often kept and reused several times over.

The usual method of selling bread in Bristol was through women known as 'hucksters'. They were allowed a penny in the shilling profit for their labour and their rights were protected in a city ordinance, dated 1473, which forbade anyone else to sell bread: 'no maner of brede to be put to sale but that hit be delivered without colour or collusion to the Hucksters of Bristow'. Similarly, women brewed and sold ale, and there were strict regulations to ensure quality and that true measure was given. Traders tended to stick together, as in Butcher's Row, Fish Street, Corn Street, Milk Street or Bread Street. Their shops were tightly packed and each had a sign hanging outside to advertise their wares; a knife for a cutler, a bushel on a pole for freshly brewed ale and a cook's flesh hook and ladle for a cookshop. Bristol's six cookshops congregated in Cockyn (Cook's) Row in the High Street. They sold ready-prepared and cooked hot food such as roast meats, pies, sauces and puddings or offered cooking services to customers supplying some or all of the ingredients. Prices were carefully regulated and varied according to who provided the ingredients.

Each cookshop had a narrow frontage to the street with an open hearth and oven. The Town Council carried out a survey of its cookshops and reported that two had hearths at the front of the shop, encroaching on the street, where cauldrons of meat were stewing while joints were being roasted on a spit over an open fire. Three of them had 'dressing boards' where the food was prepared which also encroached onto the street. The enticing smell of cooking wafting around the streets drew in hungry customers to purchase dishes of roast, fried or boiled meat, fish, game, fowl, geese, rabbit and small birds. Although there were specialist pie bakers, some of Bristol's cookshops also had an oven in which to bake pies; customers could bring their own meat and have it made into a hot pie, such as '1½ d for paste, fire and trouble upon a capon'.

With so much ready-to-eat food available in the streets, there would have been huge temptation for cheats, unsavoury dealers and dishonest cooks. All kinds of tricks and deceptions were practised on the unwary customer: loaves of bread were sold with stones to make them heavier; pie makers cheated with their fillings; bakers added inferior grain, and even sand; ale houses served watered-down ales; and spicerers stocked packs of pounded spices mixed with common seeds. Meat was sold when it had become putrid, wine when it had turned sour, bread when it had gone green. Pepper was sold damp to make it swell and weigh more and a sack of rotten oats might have some handfuls of fresh oats placed in the top of the sack. It is hardly surprising that, rather than risk being cheated by the baker with short-weight loaves of poor-grade flour, many made up their own dough for him to bake in his oven. Buying ready-prepared hot dishes from the cookshops could also be hazardous, which may be why some customers chose to supply their own ingredients. If they had no spit or oven but could afford some meat, a housewife would send a meat pie stamped with her initials to the local bakery, which may be the origin of the nursery rhyme:

Pat-a-Cake, Pat-a-Cake, Baker's Man,
Bake me a Cake as fast as you can.
Pat it and Prick it and mark it with B,
And put it in the oven for baby and me.

Like most traders, Bristol cookshops had their own guild, which was intended to control and protect their own specialist business. Trade regulations were rigorous and every town had a trading organisation which controlled who could and could not trade freely, so no one could encroach upon another's business and no shopkeeper could deal in goods made by men of other trades: no carpenter could work as a joiner; no butcher could sell cooked meat; no victualler could bake bread for sale; no one but a butcher could slaughter even a pig. The hours of work, rates of pay and number of journeymen employed by a master were fixed. Men entering the town to sell their goods were looked upon with great suspicion. They were 'strangers' or 'foreigners', and their activities were carefully supervised in the interests of the town's citizens. Taxes, levies and dues were commonplace as well as complicated: shippers and traders were charged a wide variety of fees, such as pantage (for maintenance of a bridge), stallage (for a stall in the market), pavage (road maintenance), lastage (storage), wharfage and cranage. Some towns, including Bristol, endorsed restrictive practices and banned the trading of certain goods by outsiders altogether.

In Bristol, the control of food and wine was linked to power, and it was most often shipowners and merchants who rose to positions of authority, which they held onto for several centuries. So, in 1552, a royal charter from Edward VI was granted to 'The Master, Wardens and Commonality of Merchant Venturers of the City of Bristol' – a body that is still influential in Bristol. The city was run by a more or less self-elected clique of councillors and aldermen, led by a mayor and a sheriff – mostly rich merchants who dominated city life. The authorities imposed a whole range of standards and regulations to try to prevent price fixing, unfair competition, food adulteration and weight cheats. But they were really more interested in creaming off as much as possible through taxes and levies by preventing food traders from making undue profits, failing to pay levies or unfairly competing with others.

There was also at the time some genuine concern about hygiene and the sale of unwholesome food: cookshops were forbidden to serve reheated meat 'on pain of a penalty of half a mark' or to 'caste no stinking water in the High Street'; butchers and fishmongers were forbidden to sell meat or fish more than two days old or display their wares by murky candlelight; cookshops could not sell raw fish as that would compete with fishmongers, who in turn were forbidden to cry 'salt fish and herring' during certain hours so that salt-fish hawkers could sell their cured fish around the streets without competition. Certain fresh fish could only be bought from fishing boats along the riverbank or shellfish from the cockle women on Welsh Back. Salmon, however, might be sold in the High Street – and so on.

Market days always attracted pickpockets, thieves and cheats. Food adulterers and weight cheats were tried by the *Piepoudre* Court and immediately punished. Taken from the Norman French, *Pie*, or *pied*, meant foot and *poudre* meant powder; the expression roughly meant 'dusty feet' or ragamuffin. Start-

The initial letter from an old Bristol charter illustrates a prison for wrongdoers and the punishment for cheating bakers

ing in 1483, the Court convened every market day under an oak tree on Old Market and later, the legend goes, the pub – the Stag and Hounds – was built on the site and the Court was then held in an upstairs room inside the pub. There was an annual ceremony to mark the Court's opening in which food and drink were served, but rowdies who had downed too much free ale and cider often spoiled the proceedings, so by 1870 the boozing was banned (though the old pub is still open for business). If a felon was found guilty he was given a swift and public punishment: a baker caught selling short-weight or bad bread would be dragged through the streets on a hurdle and then placed in a pillory with an offending loaf hung around his neck; a butcher selling bad meat was similarly pilloried and the rotten meat was burned under him; a vintner found selling sour wine was forced to drink a draught of it and the rest poured over his head as he sat in the pillory – so everyone could see that justice was being done.

Life was far from dull in medieval Bristol, and there were numerous religious holidays, fairs and pageants to look forward to. The eve of St Catherine's Day in November was the most important festival for the weavers, and the mayor and members of the Corporation were entertained in the Weavers' Hall, near Temple Church (off Victoria Street), with spiced cake, bread and wine – 'the cups merrily filled about the house' – before returning to their homes, 'ready to receive at their doors St Katherine's players, making them to drink at their doors, and rewarding them for their plays'. Every town dweller liked to get out into the streets to enjoy a spectacle and an excuse to feast and drink. The members of each guild (practically every working citizen belonged to a guild) assembled to join in a splendid procession through the streets with music, flags and banners. The Corporation provided gallons of wine and covered the muddy streets with layers of sand. Members of trade companies dressed up in gay clothes and marched in procession through the streets with torches. The afternoon of saints' days was often spent in sports and games or watching an open-air performance of miracle plays, in which every craft claimed its special part. Other distractions were travelling companies of play actors, Morris dancing, minstrels, jugglers, acrobats, puppeteers, rope walkers and bear and bull baiting. Even executions provided free entertainment; there being no carts in Bristol, the condemned had to walk on foot, cheered on by the crowd, along the long road from the prison at Newgate, north of the Castle, to Cotham at the top of St Michael's Hill, the traditional location for hangings at the time. Along the route, street hawkers and cookshops did a roaring trade in hot food and ale houses were full to bursting.

Cakes, biscuits and sweetmeats always appeared at civic occasions, especially traditional feasts. Christmas Eve to Twelfth Night was a period of 'unlimited guzzling' with feasting, drinking and entertainments. Enriched spiced cakes such as simnels or cracknels were often baked for special occasions to be drunk with ale or mead. In 1478, the accounts of St Ewen's church, Bristol, recorded these ingredients for some cakes for a church feast:

A bushel of meal for cakes …
Item for saffron for the same cakes
Item for milk and cream
Item for eggs to the same

The flour was most likely first baked in the oven in an earthen pot, then sieved, and then:

take clotted cream or sweet butter, but cream is best, then take sugar, cloves, mace, saffron, and yolks of eggs, so much as will seem to season your flour, then put these things into the cream, temper all together, then put thereto your flour so make your cakes, the paste will be very short, therefore make them very little, lay paper under them.

At the Bristol celebration for Corpus Christi, when Mystery Plays were performed, invited citizens were offered spiced cakebread, sugar wafers, apples and wine – all paid for by the mayor and sheriff. When perambulations of the town boundaries took place, the mayor and sheriff partook of a breakfast

A Great Mortality

The people certainly knew how to enjoy themselves, except during periods of extreme hardship, famine or plague. The Plague or Black Death, then known as the 'Great Mortality', reached Bristol on 15 August 1348 and 'extended its ravages' to Gloucester, then swept east to Oxford and south to London. Whole villages were wiped out and some religious houses lost all their inmates. But the worst affected were the large towns, with their filthy and congested housing where people and rats lived close together. In Bristol, existing graveyards were soon overflowing with the dead and new graves had to be dug elsewhere. Trade came to a standstill and grass grew inches high in Broad Street and High Street. When the plague had finally passed, things were very different. An acute labour shortage meant survivors could find work where they chose and demand higher rewards for their services, and the guilds lost some of their authority.

consisting of seven quarts of wine and two pennyworth of cakes, and after visiting the 'Shire Stones' – an 'afternoon of drinking' – disposed of a further gallon of Madeira.

By the fifteenth century, Bristol was so prosperous that the merchant-shipowners had begun to help build superb churches such as St Stephen and St Mary Redcliffe, 'whose noble spire could serve as a guide for any ship floating up on the flood tide'. They had also diverted the river Frome from its lower course to St Augustine's Marsh and built a stone quay (the Key) against which seagoing ships could safely moor when grounded at low tide. The Key became the principal place for ships to lade and discharge. There was another stone quay on the larger Avon, below Bristol Bridge at St Nicholas' Back, and each had its own custom house.

The extravagant demands of large Norman households and the increasingly prospering city people kick-started Bristol merchants into venturing further afield in search of exotic ingredients – especially dried cod, spices, sugar and wine. It was the beginning of Bristol's long and hugely profitable involvement in the food trade.

ALL AT SEA

On a brisk morning in October 1430, William Cruez, master of the *Marie Bird*, was hove-to in the Kingroad, an anchorage at the mouth of the river Avon. The captain had made a fast crossing from Bordeaux, where he had sold large consignments of Bristol cloth and tanned hides to French dealers in exchange for more than 80 'tuns in pipes or hogsheads' of the new season's pressing of Gascon wine, which was eagerly awaited by 46 Bristol and London shareholders. Master Cruez could see coming up the flapping sails of the Irish ship the *Agnes* as she arrived from her regular run between Bristol and Waterford, in Ireland. She too had sailed out with a cargo of Bristol cloth, which in Ireland had been exchanged for barrels of salt cod, white herring, salmon and hake. Closing behind them were 12 other ships on the Bordeaux-Bristol wine run, with one or two stragglers still turning into the safety of the Bristol Channel.

WINE
Every autumn, after the grape harvest, these large convoys of Bristol ships set out for Gascon ports, their holds filled with woollen cloth and hides which they exchanged with the French for thousands of pipes and barrels of white wine called Claret. This was the busiest period; a season fraught with storms when shipwrecks were often plundered by coastal communities. Piracy was a year-round threat, with French, Italian and Spanish pirates lying in wait for such a valuable prize. During the endless periods of war, Bristol ships had to carry extra armed crewmen as guards or travel in convoys. Captain Cruez and his men preferred the summer, when the wine runs stopped and Bristol ships were sent to Iceland, where they spent several months trading for the freeze-dried cod called stockfish.

On the banks of the river Avon, close by the Kingroad anchorage, a community of pilots and oarsmen lived in the village of Crockern Pill and made their living towing these huge ships up the tortuous seven miles of river. Known as 'hobblers', they were skilled in catching the tide and navigating tight river bends and the narrow, dramatic cliffs of the Avon gorge. For the crews of these ships it was like venturing into a strange, interior world far from the open sea. As they were towed around the final sharp turn in the river, mariners were suddenly met with the sight of a great town, with the outlines of St Mary Redcliffe and the priory of St Augustine rising above a skyline crammed with the roofs of houses and warehouses. As they reached the new 'Key' on the Frome and threw out their lines, an army of stevedores, wharfmen and merchants were waiting, ready to unload their valuable cargo.

By the fifteenth century, Bristol was the third largest town in England and the second most important port. Shipbuilding had become an important business and several men now owned their own fleet of ships, which they leased to merchants. The biggest player was William Canynges (the Younger), a hugely wealthy cloth-maker and exporter, who turned to shipping and owned 10 vessels from 500 to a mighty 900 tons. William Worcestre, Bristol's local historian, recorded that 'Master Canynges, who was mayor five times in eight years, kept 800 men employed in maritime occupations, and every day had labourers, masons and carpenters etc. to the number of 100 men.' Apart from occasional royal command for these ships to serve as men of war, for most of the year the Bristol fleet was kept busy on routine export/import runs. Bristol and the surrounding Cotswolds made up the most important cloth-making region in the country, and the city also had flourishing tannery, pottery and glass-making businesses, which had expanded into a mini industrial estate south of Bristol Bridge. The export of these goods was as important to the city as its imports of wine, fish, salt, olive oil, iron, sugar, corn and timber. The long-established exchange trades which Bristol enjoyed with France, Ireland and Iceland were central to the city's economy. But that was all about to change.

In 1453, at the end of the Hundred Years War, the French seized Bordeaux. The English were expelled from Gascony and the interdependent cloth and wine trade, vital to Bristol's economy, seemed doomed. In spite of stringent new French regulations and taxes, however, Gascon and Bristol wine merchants managed to retain some of their lucrative trade. As one French merchant said: 'How could our poor people subsist when they could not sell their wines or procure English merchandise?' Numerous Bordeaux merchants settled in Bristol rather than live under French rule. Nevertheless, several Bristol merchants turned their attentions to alternative markets farther south. The Spanish and Portuguese became keen purchasers of English cloth, and by the 1490s half of Bristol's cloth was shipped to Iberia and traded for Spanish white wine or 'sack' such as malmsey and a sherry sack from Andalusia which was to become uniquely identified with Bristol. Sweet wines, including Madeira, were bought from the Portuguese. By the end of the century, Iberian wines made up one-third of Bristol's wine imports and became hugely popular in England.

SPICES

Trading in the Mediterranean brought Bristol ships into contact with dealers selling all kinds of exotic luxury goods brought in by Arab traders on the overland routes from Asia and India. Bristol ships began to bring home large consignments of olive oil, wax, honey, almonds, saffron, liquorice, vinegar, salt, cork and citrus fruits, plus small quantities of spices and sugar. But the port of London was still the dominant dealer in these goods. London monopolies and the many trade restrictions abroad would continue to hamper the efforts of Bristol merchants to get in on the act.

This was a time of rivalry and upheaval in the Near East, where the spice routes from India and Africa converged. The Ottoman invasion was advancing steadily on Constantinople, the Turks were moving in on the Black Sea and a rival Catalan fleet menaced the Western Mediterranean – while the Italian citystates of Venice and Genoa kept their stranglehold on the Mediterranean spice markets. Anyone wishing to import sugar and spices into their country had no option but to buy through Venetian and Genoese traders, who acted as middlemen and took a hefty cut from the purchase price. As long as this persisted, the price of sugar and spices in Europe would remain high. Traders in northern Europe had long wanted to break the monopoly; London and Bristol merchants were desperate to cut through these barriers and trade direct.

Robert Sturmy was a Bristol merchant who had been giving the problem considerable thought. He had made a fortune supplying the king's forces in France during the Hundred Years War and become a prosperous and respected figure in the political and commercial elite of Bristol. The plan he came up with was ambitious, expensive, courageous and foolhardy. But it almost worked and it opened the way to new thinking about venturing beyond the restricted areas of trade to which Bristol merchants had hitherto been confined.

In the winter of 1444, Sturmy obtained export permits to send a large shipment of wool and tin to Pisa. Several wealthy city merchants, such as William Canynges, invested in the project. But it is believed that Sturmy's real plan was to sail on to the North African coast, where he would quietly load up with pepper and ginger bought direct from Arab dealers. Possibly to avoid suspicion, he also gave passage to 160 pilgrims bound for Jaffa Port, then in Eygpt, where they were disembarked and where the ship took on her secret cargo. But this may not be the whole story; it is also thought that Sturmy may have hoped to break into another quite different trade monopoly for a product which was particularly valuable to Bristol's cloth-making industry. Alum was a chemical compound essential for fixing dyes on fine cloth. The Turks controlled the alum mines of Asia Minor and the only other source was on the island of Chios in the Aegean, which was controlled by the Genoese. It is possible that Sturmy had hatched ambitious plans to bring back cargos of both pepper and alum. But he was successful with neither for, as his ship was sailing homewards along the coast of Greece, it was caught in a sudden gale, driven onto the rocks and dashed to pieces. All of her crew perished, 'to the extreme grief of their wives and their friends in Bristol'.

Despite this terrible setback, Sturmy continued to dream of breaking into the spice and/or alum trade. In 1457, financed by a group of shareholders with a licence from Henry VI to export colossal amounts of tin, lead, wool and cloth, he loaded his own ship, the *Katherine Sturmy*, and two support vessels. Before departing on his second voyage, Sturmy signed a will in which he wrote that he placed great hopes in the commercial success of his 'monumental undertaking, calculating that his total wealth would double in value if his ships returned safely to port'. This time, Sturmy sailed on the *Katherine* himself and successfully reached 'divers parts of the Levant' as well as the Aegean islands, where he sold his cargo and loaded up with either spices or alum or both. But the Genoese had got wind of his business and were determined that the *Katherine* should never reach home. A Greek-Genoese freebooter called Guiliano Gattilusio lay in wait for Sturmy near Malta and, 'after a wild pursuit on the high seas', viciously attacked the English ships 'with cannons, catapults, crossbows, grapnels and sorts of weapons'. The attack prompted outrage in England and all Genoese merchants in London were arrested, incarcerated in the Fleet Prison and had their goods confiscated until they paid the enormous sum of £6,000 in compensation to Sturmy and his shareholders. But Robert Sturmy was already dead; either he perished during the attack or died soon after, a disappointed and probably ruined man.

Although they suffered huge losses, the English shareholders in this disastrous venture do not seem to have been entirely put off. The spark lit by Sturmy continued to smoulder in Bristol's commercial ambitions until some 20 years later, when it took hold once again and fired up the search for different products in a different sea – this time it was for cod and sugar and the urge to find new land in the Atlantic.

COD

During the period when Robert Sturmy had been struggling to break the Genoese stranglehold on the spice and alum trade in the south, Bristol merchants were also battling with other powerful forces determined to hinder trading for fish in the north. Fast days in the Middle Ages, when only fish was permitted, meant a regular and profitable trade in fish. Since Bristol had no fishing fleet of its own, it relied on trading with Ireland for its major source of fish – as a local proverb confirms:

> Herring of Sligo and salmon of Bann,
> Has made in Bristol many a rich man.

But England's voracious demand for fish meant dealers had to look further afield to supplement the regular Irish supplies. Herring and cod were the two most abundant and important species of fish in the Middle Ages, though neither was eaten fresh – they were salted, dried or smoked. The bulk of herring was to be found in the North and Baltic Seas and herring for the English markets came in through the east-coast ports, where it was quickly cured. The major cod fisheries, however, were mostly found far out in the North Atlantic and around the coasts of Norway and Iceland. Dried cod – stockfish or *stokfish* – was still Bristol's most important food. It was the staple diet for the poor, it supplemented the shortage of meat and it was also consumed by almost everyone during fish and fast days. Early-spring shoals of cod were caught, gutted and hung out on sticks to dry (hence, possibly, the

Preparing salted and dried cod

Salt or dried cod required long soaking in several changes of water, followed by lengthy simmering (boiling was said to harden it even more). The commonly eaten dried stockfish was like a piece of hard board and needed a long preparation time. A later recipe by John Collins, from 1681, gives an idea of what was entailed:

> Beat it soundly with Mallet for half an hour or more and lay it three days a soaking, then Boyle it on a simmering Fire about an hour, with as much water as will cover it till it be soft, then take it up and put in butter, eggs, and Mustard champed together …

Collins suggests serving the fish with boiled and buttered potatoes or parsnips. But as potatoes were not known in England until the sixteenth century, medieval recipes would have used parsnips, which helped counter the strong, rather high flavour of the fish. Other recipes suggest cooking in milk, or putting root vegetables, rice or pulses in the liquor to help absorb the salt and improve the flavour and texture of the fish.

name) along the coast in the cold, dry air to a point at which they would keep almost indefinitely.

The relationship between Bristol and Iceland went back a long way. Bristol ships took essential supplies of salt, flour, malt, butter, honey, pots and pans, woollen cloth and other household necessities to Iceland, which had few natural resources of its own. All the Bristol dealers wanted in return was fish, which Icelandic fishermen caught and cured in massive quantities. But fish dealers in the North Atlantic were about to confront the all-powerful Hanseatic League.

The Hanseatic League, or *Hanse* (a medieval German word for 'guild' or 'association'), was formed in the thirteenth century in the north German port of Lübeck, to protect and regulate trade in northern Europe, including the herring fisheries. For many years the Hanse had stood up to the flouting of its rules by monarchs, fought piracy, dredged channels, erected lighthouses, trained pilots and built and sold ships. But their power over trading concessions, tariffs and monopolies had become too great. Having successfully monopolised the herring trade, the Hanse now attempted to do the same with cod. The Hanse started to notice Bristol activities in Iceland and tried to control them. Differences between them reached boiling point and in 1475 the Hanse ports blocked Bristol merchants from buying Icelandic cod. Once again, Bristol's comfortable trading arrangements were being threatened by new political and economic problems. If its merchants were to keep making profits, they would need to get ahead of the game and seek out power bases of their own.

Into the story of this search steps John Jay junior, a wealthy shipowner and one-time sheriff of Bristol. Like many people at the time, he believed that somewhere in the Atlantic was an unexplored island called Hy-Brasil, a legendary place often depicted on early charts. One Celtic story puts the island some way off the west coast of Ireland and in Gaelic the name means 'Isle of the Blest'. Italian and Portuguese maps, perhaps predictably, put the island to the north of Madeira and west of the Azores. But John Jay and his business colleagues were not interested in an island of enchantment. What they dreamed of finding in the Atlantic was new land.

There are a number of ideas as to why Bristolians were prepared to invest huge sums and their best ships in the search for this mythical island. One theory suggests that they were looking for a new fishing base to replace the now-inaccessible Icelandic fisheries. What was needed was a stretch of coastal land with drying winds, easy landing and a safe anchorage. The island of Hy-Brasil, if it existed, could be ideal. It was no secret that the Basque fleets had found limitless quantities of huge cod far out in the North Atlantic that they were bringing home ready-cured. To do this, they must have had access to land on which to process the fish – so where was it? Centuries earlier, Viking ships had made landfall on the extreme north-west reaches of the Atlantic and it is generally thought that the Basque fishermen had also found the rocky shores of what is now called Newfoundland. Were they selling their salt cod to Bristol ships and had they told the ships' captains about their wonderful new land? There is little archive evidence to support this theory, but if you say 'cod' to a Bristolian today, they will tell you some variant on this story – and they may be right.

SUGAR

There was, however, another possibility apart from the cod connection. Since 1466, Bristol customs records show small but regular shipments of sugar arriving via Lisbon from Portuguese Madeira. The island had been discovered early in the century by the Portuguese explorer Henry the Navigator, who believed that the conditions there were ideal for cultivating sugar cane. John Jay, and his fellow merchants whose ships regularly sailed in these waters, may have argued that if, as the Portuguese charts indicated, the island of Hy-Brasil lay near Madeira, they too might find land on which to grow their own sugar cane.

Sugar cane originated in New Guinea and spread westwards to India and Persia, where the juice, obtained by crushing the sweet pith from the bamboo-like reed, was boiled down into sugar. Through Arab traders, limited and very expensive quantities of sugar reached northern Europe, where it was used mainly as a medicine and later as a preservative for fruit. The Portuguese initiative in growing and controlling their own sugar supplies was the beginning of the great expansion of the sugar trade across the Atlantic to South America and the West Indies on the back of which was founded the Atlantic slave trade.

In July 1481, two Bristol ships, the *Trinity* and the *George*, were made ready for a long voyage. John Jay's principal partner in this venture was Thomas Croft, a wealthy Bristol customs official who wrote that they 'set forth not by cause of merchaundise but thentent to serce and fynd a certain Ile called the Isle of Brasile'. The previous summer they had sent a smaller ship, but after a few weeks it was turned back by storms and forced to put into harbour along the Irish coast. Despite this setback, Croft, Jay and several other merchants considered it worth investing enormous sums and two of the city's best and finest ships in another, larger expedition. The master of the *Trinity*, John Lloyd, was described as 'the most scientific mariner in all England' – so the project had at its disposal the best navigational skills for finding land, if there was any to be found. They loaded 40 bushels (about 1 metric ton) of salt into the holds and set out on 15 July. But where were they heading – north or south?

The *Trinity* and the *George* regularly plied between Bristol, Spain, Portugal and Madeira and were licensed to export huge cargos of cloth and to import wine, Spanish iron, olive oil, fruit, honey, vinegar, rosin, cloth dyes, wax and sugar. All this sea trading inevitably led to an exchange of ideas and experiences between sailors with a common interest in the Atlantic and Bristol sailors heard a good deal of sea lore: 'the sea air of late is laden with stories of lost unknown lands across the Ocean'. So did the ships head into the South Atlantic rather than the North Atlantic? After many weeks at sea, both ships returned safely to Bristol. But there is no record of where they went or what they found or if they returned loaded or empty-handed. Whether their reason for seeking an 'Isle of Brasile' was for new land on which they could establish sugar plantations, or windswept coastlines where they could process cod, remains a mystery. The far-sighted activities of Bristol men such as Sturmy and Jay, however, left a legacy of innovation, courage and determination. According to the Spanish Ambassador in England, every year from then on Bristol sent four or five ships to search for this elusive land. Certainly the earlier loss of Gascony, the serious blow dealt to the fish trade with Iceland and the struggle to break into spice and sugar trades had spurred them on to search for new outlets elsewhere. It was in this continuing climate of optimism that Bristol merchants welcomed a new proposition from a Venetian explorer when he came to their city around 15 years later. His name was John Cabot.

CABOT AND NEW LANDS

It is believed that John Cabot was born Zuan Chabotto around 1451, the same year as his rival Christopher Columbus, and that both men came from Genoa. But when John was 10 years old, the family moved to Venice, where he went to sea and served on spice-carrying ships. He soon acquired a reputation as 'a very good mariner' with 'a fine mind greatly skilled in navigation'. By this time the Turks had taken control of the Mediterranean routes and it was clear that trying to procure direct trade in spices with the East via the Mediterranean was no longer possible. Perhaps there was another way.

Portugal became the first country to find an alternative route to Asia via Africa when Vasco da Gama rounded the Cape, continued eastwards and sailed across the Indian Ocean to South India. Meanwhile, Christopher Columbus had developed a different plan entirely; he believed he could reach the Indies by sailing west across the South Atlantic. He eventually managed to persuade the Spanish crown to fund him and in 1492 made land on an island which he believed to be Asia and called it the 'West Indies' – it was, in fact, Cuba. He returned triumphantly to Spain and later made several more

With his small ship the *Matthew* ready to sail, Cabot and crew take their leave of the burghers of Bristol. Painting by Thomson, from J.A. Cochrane, *The Story of Newfoundland* (Montreal 1938)

voyages to the region, including the mainland of South America, thus making him the first European to discover the Americas, although he never accepted it was not Asia.

John Cabot was determined to find the Atlantic route to Asia that his rival Columbus had failed to locate. Unable to raise any interest from backers in southern Europe, he moved with his wife and children to Bristol in 1495. It had occurred to him that England, being at the end of the spice line and paying the highest prices, would be interested in finding a short, high-latitude spice route direct to the Indies which would make a fortune for England. Having heard stories about expeditions from Bristol in search of land to the far north-west of the Atlantic, Cabot drew up his own plan and sent it to the English king. Henry VII had turned Columbus down and so missed the chance to be among the first to profit from his discoveries. So, on 5 March 1496, he gave royal consent for Cabot to sail westward with up to five ships 'to find, discover and investigate whatsoever islands, countries, regions or provinces of heathens and infidels, in whatsoever part of the world, places which before this time were unknown to all Christians'. Here Cabot was to 'set up our banner and ensigns' in any land that the expedition discovered and to 'subdue, occupy and possess' those lands in the king's name. Henry had agreed to Cabot's voyage so long as he did not have to fund him and could take one-fifth of any profits made in kind or cash. But it was made clear that Cabot was 'bound and holden to return only to Bristow' – a vital factor for his Bristol backers as it meant the city would become the major port of the spice trade, bypassing the Levant and rivalling London, Antwerp and Lisbon. All that Robert Sturmy had hoped for and more would have been gained.

Cabot sailed on 20 May 1497, on a small vessel called the *Matthew* with a crew of 18 men. After sailing west for 35 days, the *Matthew* made landfall at a spot where the crew found signs of human habitation, including snares and fishing nets and swarms of fierce mosquitoes, but no sign of humans themselves. The seas were teeming with cod and the crew brought up basketfuls of enormous fish. Three months later, Cabot returned to Bristol in triumph, claiming a 'Newfoundland'. He immediately raced to London to report to the king.

Cabot left no detailed record of the voyage and most of our knowledge of what he found and experienced comes from contemporary descriptions in letters written home by Italians in London who, as soon as Cabot arrived in the capital, would have met with him and heard about his trip. Raimondo Soncino, Milanese envoy in London, immediately sent official reports to the Duke of Milan, and Lorenzo Pasqualigo, a merchant based in London, wrote to his brothers in Venice on 23 August. One extraordinary piece of evidence, not found until 500 years after Cabot's voyage, was a letter written by an English merchant called John Day, a rather slippery character with several irons in the fire, who for several years had been trading between England and Spain. Day lived in Seville, where he was trying to curry favour with Christopher Columbus, who was then preparing to go on further expeditions. Day, who was often in Bristol around the time Cabot returned in the *Matthew*, seems to have picked up considerable navigational data about Cabot's voyage, which he passed on in great detail to Columbus. Whilst playing down the importance of the voyage, Day also gave a valuable picture of Cabot's experiences, including the information that the expedition 'found many fish of the kind that in Iceland are cured in the air and sell in England and other countries and which in England are called stockfish'. Cabot, Day wrote, had found a land rich in pasturage, with tall trees and much evidence of human habitation but had encountered no humans. There is, however, something in the letter that is particularly significant to the Bristol story:

> It is considered certain that this same point of land at another time was found and discovered by those of Bristol who found *el Brasil* as you are already aware, which is called *Ysla de Brasil*, and is presumed and believed to be the *tierra firma* which those of Bristol discovered.

This tantalising remark suggests that one of the many Bristol ships searching for land in the Atlantic had made landfall – even before Cabot.

News of Cabot's voyage created a sensation in Bristol. The king gave him £10 as a reward and an annuity of £20, paid for by Bristol customs. Cabot is reported to have 'swaggered about … in gay, silken apparel and the common people run after him like madmen'. He immediately set about preparations for a second voyage, and in February 1498 the king issued new letters patent for a return voyage to the 'New Found Land'. Cabot, who believed that he had discovered the source of the 'spices of the world', planned to set up a colony from which to trade. In May he set out with five ships, a year's provisions and 'course Cloth, Capes, Laces, Points and other Trifles' for the native people, supplied by Bristol merchants keen to get in on the new potential trade. A few days later, one of the ships put into an Irish port in distress; the other four were not expected home for at least a month. But they never returned.

Three years after Cabot's mysterious disappearance, Gaspar Corte Real, an explorer from the Azores, made landfall on Newfoundland; his men captured some Beothuk Indians and returned with them to Lisbon. (Like Cabot, Corte Real himself failed to return from his expedition.) The Beothuk Indians had in their possession a broken gilt sword of Italian make and a pair of silver earrings stamped 'made in Venice', which could only have come from Cabot. This offers intriguing possibilities but no plausible explanation for his disappearance. His first voyage was certainly the forerunner to the English colonisation of North America, but like Columbus, Cabot never learned the significance or value of his discoveries.

But this was not the end of Bristol's involvement in the 'Golden Age' of maritime exploration and the creation of English colonies in the New World. Some Bristolians stubbornly persisted in their belief in a north-west passage to the spice markets and continued to fund exploratory voyages in the North Atlantic. A few even set out on their own ships, but failed in their objectives or to return at all. Although Henry VIII had not been keen on maritime ventures, Elizabeth I was an enthusiastic supporter and during her reign several of her wealthiest Bristol subjects invested in major ventures. The Wynter family of Bristol subscribed to several, including Martin Frobisher's three expeditions and Francis Drake's voyage around the world. Bristol investors expected a return on their money in the form of merchandise and

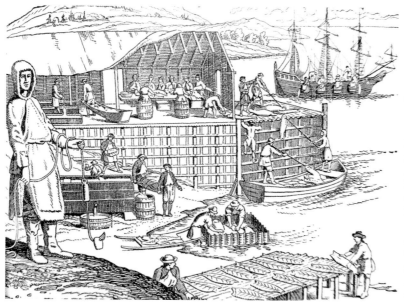

'The Manner of Fishing for, Curing, and Drying Cod.' Detail of Herman Mollo's so-called Codfish Map, from *The World Described* (1715). Courtesy of the Public Archives of Canada

new trade opportunities and a young member of the Wynter family was sent with Drake's fleet to keep an eye on their interests. But Bristol merchants were not really interested in exploration for its own sake, being more concerned with increasing markets and profits than on gaining a place in the history books.

Although they never found a new spice route to Asia, Bristol men could claim to have played a major role in founding colonies in the West Indies, America and what is now Canada. The established cod fisheries off Newfoundland and New England were reported to 'teem with flounder which can be speared as fast as you can take up fritters with a sharp stick, and as many lobsters can be caught in a few hours as will feed a hundred men for a day'. This sort of news spread along the Bristol quays; companies were set up and bigger ships built and sent out to establish new land bases. Looking forward briefly to the seventeenth century, it was in 1610 that John Guy, a prominent Bristol merchant associated with a joint stock venture established by Bristol and London merchants, set out to create what is now considered the first permanent English settlement at Cupid's Grove, in Newfoundland. Its charter stated that its purpose was 'to secure and make safe the trade of fishing … and reserve the best fishing "rooms" for English crews'. Thirty-nine male colonists, led by John Guy, set out from Bristol with instructions that included fortifying a settlement, trading with the local Indian people and converting them to Christianity, collecting mineral-ore samples, fishing and trading in cured fish, and obtaining oil from whale blubber or the fat of seals and walruses.

The first two winters at Cupid's Grove were mild, with relatively few deaths, and the colonists fulfilled their instructions quite well. Guy sailed home to Bristol in 1611 with tales of a friendly climate and some great successes and in 1612 arrived back in Newfoundland with 16 female settlers. In the spring of 1613, as a letter home from Guy reported, the first settler baby was born. But there were problems with climate and the soil: vegetables grew but grain did not, and there was insufficient hay to feed animals through the hard winters. For a while, the colonists had successfully traded and exchanged gifts with the Beothuk people, but these good relations did not last, plus the settlers were constantly threatened by pirates. John Guy's attempt ultimately proved a failure, partly due to his inability to exert his authority over the pirates, who used the island for refitting, and partly to the refusal of fishermen from ports other than Bristol and London to accept his authority. Later, in 1618, John Barker and some members of the Society of Merchant Venturers of Bristol bought land on the west coast of Conception Bay and founded the colony of Bristol Hope, which boasted many houses and a fine harbour. This colony appears to have been successful and a further strong link binding Bristol and Newfoundland was forged.

The principal aim of Bristol merchants was to have control over their own enterprises rather than to settle colonial communities, and it was not until 1681, when William Penn established the Quaker colony of Pennsylvania (where slavery was forbidden) that Bristol finally supported a venture not primarily driven by trading interests. Nevertheless, men who sailed out to discover and colonise the North American continent were largely Bristolians, financed in Bristol and sailing from Bristol. By the end of the seventeenth century, the foundations of England's colonies in America had been laid, much of it by the determination and funds of Bristol people. The first town in America named Bristol was founded in New England in 1632 by Robert Aldworth, one of the richest and best-connected Bristol merchants of his generation. Today there are more than 25 Bristols in America.

The Elizabethan Era

ELIZABETH I'S ROYAL PROGRESS TO BRISTOL

The bells of St Stephen's church in Bristol pealed loudly and the townspeople, dressed in their Sunday best, cheered and jostled for a good position from which to view their queen. Heavy, late-summer storms had put the Royal progress from Windsor to Bristol well behind schedule, and when she finally reached Bristol on 15 August 1574, Queen Elizabeth I composed a prayer of thanksgiving 'for preserving me in this long and dangerous journey'. Accompanied by an enormous retinue, the queen was met at Lawford's Gate – which led from Bristol Castle to Old Market – by the Mayor of Bristol, carrying the sword of state, and his aldermen in their bright red gowns, all guarded by 300 local soldiers who occasionally fired into the air in celebration. Curiously dressed orators suddenly appeared before the procession to declaim flattering verses to Her Majesty. At the City Cross, an 'excellent boye' dressed as Fame made a speech of welcome:

> No sooner was pronounced the name, but babes in street 'gan leap,
> The youth, the age, the rich, the poor, came running all on heap,
> And, clapping hands, cried mainly out, 'O blessed is the hour!
> Our Queen is coming to the town, with princely train and power.'

He threw a garland into the air to the cheers of the crowd. The queen smiled graciously and waved to her subjects. She was demonstrating a sixteenth-century version of the royal walkabout.

Royal progresses were not new; several monarchs had used them to raise funds for depleted royal coffers. Henry VII, who was especially keen to squeeze as much money as he could from his wealthier subjects, visited Bristol in 1490 and, after being lavishly entertained, cast covetous eyes on the richest citizens. He noted 'how their wives were so finely dressed' and slapped a 5-per-cent fine on the properties of anyone worth more than £20. The richest Bristolians reluctantly paid up, knowing that if they refused, the king's men would take what they wanted by force.

Every summer, throughout her long reign, Elizabeth I made a practice of taking her court on royal progresses through her kingdom. It was an opportunity to assert her authority, to see and be seen around the country and remind everyone that she was in charge. For her hosts, whether civic dignitaries or landed aristocrats, it was a chance to strengthen ties with the crown and win favours. Everyone with ambition to further themselves and their position dreamed of entertaining royalty, but the costs were enormous and the queen's refusal of an invitation, or failure to turn up even when she had accepted, was often done deliberately to punish or make a political point and could result in considerable financial cost and loss of face.

Bristow had by now been renamed 'Bristoll' and had become a town of considerable importance and wealth, with a cathedral and the beautiful church of St Mary Redcliffe – which, on her visit, the queen described as 'the goodliest, fairest and most famous parish church in England'. The people were keen to impress their queen and the processional route was spruced up. Elaborate plans were made for pageants, speeches of welcome and entertainments. A three-day mock sea battle on the rivers Avon and Frome was planned and the Marsh (now Queen Square) between the rivers was covered in thick layers of sand and a special raised gallery erected on it from which the queen could sit and view the dramatic proceedings. The battle featured soldiers, sailors and numerous ships, mostly belonging to Bristol merchants, got up to look like fighting vessels sailing off in hot pursuit of one another. The total cost of supplying the soldiers with food, drink and ordnance, arming and 'dressing' the ships, hiring musicians and purchasing hundreds of yards of canvas and red cloth for special clothes was unprecedented.

The decision to pour money into a mock battle instead of the more traditional pageant was a deliberate plan to impress the queen with Bristol's military and maritime strength and its preparedness to defend queen and country. (In 1544, Bristol had sent 12 fighting ships to help the British navy lay siege to Boulogne, and later, in 1588, the town fleet made a contribution to the defeat of the Spanish Armada.) Knowing that Bristol was preparing to show off its maritime strength, the queen had ordered the Spanish ambassador to meet her there to sign a treaty which, it was hoped, would buy a few more years of peace between the two nations.

For Bristol Corporation, the total bill for entertaining Elizabeth I was over £1,000, including a gift of a silk purse containing £100 in gold coins – a very large sum in those days. Courtiers and the army of servants travelling with the royal progress were put up by townspeople or in taverns. Fortunately the Corporation did not have to pay to accommodate the queen, for she had

Queen Elizabeth I, on a royal progress, is greeted at St John's Gate, Bristol, August 1574

accepted an invitation from John Young, one of Bristol's richest citizens, to stay in his house on St Augustine's Back.

For the queen's stay, Young's 'Great House', as it was then known, underwent lavish preparations. A 40-foot-long 'presence' room, plus a little privy chamber, a warderobe and private bedroom were specially created and deco-

The queen loved hunting, which invariably began with a picnic breakfast. Owing to the disgrace of Hugh Smyth, owner of the great deer park at Ashton Court, the queen had to forego a day's hunting. Private collection

rated. The queen always brought her own bed and hangings, plus four mattresses filled with down, wool, flax and very fine feathers. On the second day of the queen's stay she attended a dinner at the Great House. It was a Friday and therefore a fish day. After Henry VIII's break with the Church of Rome, he had relaxed some fast days but Elizabeth increased them, more for political and economic reasons than religious: to reduce demand for meat, which was becoming scarce; and, since fishermen were commonly made to serve as naval sailors, to increase the fishing fleets as a source of manpower for the Royal Navy. For a royal dinner on 'fish daies' the first course might offer five or six fish dishes such as pike in sauce, minced salt salmon in a sauce of mustard, vinegar and a little sugar, smoked or pickled herring, eels, trout or roach on *sops* (bread soaked in the liquor in which the fish was cooked) tench in jelly, or a pottage of sand eels and lampreys. The second course would have featured a royal fish such as a sturgeon caught in the Severn Estuary, whale or roasted porpoise – known as the 'venison' of fish days.

After two days of watching sea battles and eating fish, the queen and her court were ready for some meatier fare and lighter entertainments. The skills of cooks (specially hired from London or even Paris) in the kitchens of the Great House were already stretched to the limit, and the bill for ingredients climbed higher and higher. The sheer range and quantity was astonishing and included birds and animals long since considered unsuitable for eating. Song birds were still popular at this time: sparrows stewed in ale with herbs and served upon sippets (small pieces of toasted bread to soak up the juices); larks cooked in wine with bone marrow, raisins, sugar and cinnamon; fruity stews of birds with fresh barberries or gooseberries; and capons boiled with bitter oranges or lemons. Some little birds were rolled up in paste and boiled as dumplings. In those days only royalty could eat swan and then only in the winter, after the breeding season. As it was summer, there could be no swan for the queen's dinner and instead there would have been a peacock 'in magnificent full feather' and roast venison with a sauce of vinegar, sugar, cinnamon and butter 'boiled together so as not to be too tart'. A roasted coney (rabbit) or hare – the head and ears left on so that it appeared lifelike – served in mustard and sugar sauce, chickens upon sorrel sops, a brace of pheasant or corncrakes with sliced onions or perhaps a curlew or bittern in a galantine sauce. (A *galauntine* or *galantyne* sauce was made with vinegar, breadcrumbs, cinnamon and other spices.) Very few vegetables were mentioned apart from spinach and sorrel, but some curious dishes of stuffed root vegetables were listed, such as carrots, turnips or cucumbers filled with a mixture of pounded liver, grated bread, chopped apple, currants, hard-boiled egg, sugar, cinnamon and ginger.

Diners could look over this rich choice and pick a little with their knife at each dish, or take a carved slice of meat or fish, prepared by the carver, and dip it into the sauce provided in small dishes called *saucers*. Quantities of cream, butter and eggs were now being used to make even richer sauces. Some were complex, with long lists of contrasting ingredients involving vinegar, spices, dried fruits and sweeteners, to recreate the medieval taste for a sweet-sour flavour which seems to have persisted. Dishes of meat and fish in jelly, aspic and galantines were especially popular because they could be coloured and shaped to excite both the eye and the palate. (Sweet fruit jellies only began to appear when pectin was discovered in the nineteenth century.) Made from various kinds of animal gelling agents, jellies were set in moulds with the elaborate shapes of flowers, herbs, trees, animals, birds and fruit, but required considerable skill to achieve the best effect.

BANQUETTING STUFFE

But all these eye-catching, rich and tasty dishes paled into insignificance when the feast reached the final 'banquet' course. The word 'banquet' in Tudor and Elizabethan times was used to describe the dessert or sweet course rather than the main feast itself. It developed from the earlier medieval dessert of spiced cakes and apples, spicy-sweet hippocras wine and wafers which Robert, Earl of Gloucester, and his guests at the castle had enjoyed after retiring to a private room whilst servants cleared the great hall ready for entertainments. By the reign of Henry VIII, a banqueting room or house was a special intimate indoor chamber, or in summer a garden pavilion or bower, where after-dinner guests could reconvene and indulge themselves with sweet wines, fruit tarts, marmalades, preserves, suckets (typically, preserved fruits) and marzipan. Like today's after-dinner guests who nibble at chocolates or fruit and nuts, the 'stuffe' of the 'banquetting' course was intended only for picking at and only the real glutton gorged upon everything, which was considered bad manners. Guests stood around drinking warmed hippocras, to aid both digestion and the mingling process, like a modern cocktail party, while the occasion also allowed the assembled to show off their gorgeous clothes. They were expected to take sweetmeats home to enjoy later, at their leisure.

Some banqueting houses were sited on the roof of the house, from where guests could cool off and admire the view. Most were in a garden setting amid a fruit-filled orchard or surrounded by borders of sweet-scented herbs and flowers, with a stream or lake nearby or vistas of the surrounding countryside. Here, people could have private conversations, listen to music and poetry, dance, carouse, play charades or watch a masque. In those days there was little privacy and the small, intimate banquet was an opportunity to let your hair down without the servants, who otherwise shadowed your every waking moment. Outdoor banqueting houses and garden recesses also offered privacy and secrecy to anyone who wanted to be alone with their lover. Indeed, according to sixteenth-century medical opinion, everything served at a banquet was designed to inflame lust. The very names of some items served at the banquet course connected them with sex, such as 'kissing comfits', 'spannish paps' of sweetened cream in the shape of breasts and elaborate sugarwork fashioned to represent gods of wine and love; there were suckets of figs which 'stere a man to venryous actes' and gingerbreads which 'provoketh sluggish husbands'; marmalades and candied sweet potato were considered aphrodisiacs to 'stir up Venus', while sweet, spiced wines made everyone 'merrie'.

During the week of the queen's visit to Bristol, the weather was very pleasant and after dinner the royal party could stroll through the steeply terraced gardens behind the Great House. Here they could admire the perfect knot gardens and, in the sheltered, sloping orchards, note new varieties of fruit and nut trees such as plums, apples, pears, walnuts, almonds, medlars, figs, peaches and cherries. John Young had started building two banqueting houses or lodges at the top end of his garden, known as the White Lodge and the Red Lodge (still on Park Row today). It is possible that they were not quite completed in time for the queen's stay and instead would have looked similar to temporary banqueting rooms or garden pavilions of the time. Rather like a modern marquee, they were covered with canvas awnings, which were painted; the walls were lined with painted and gilded wood, while there were hangings of fine embroidered fabric and silk cushions scattered about to lounge upon. The interiors were decorated with greenery and scented flowers such as jasmine and honeysuckle and the floor was strewn with rose petals. Centre-stage was an elaborately carved marble or stone table upon which was displayed a succession of extraordinarily dramatic, inventive and irresistible dishes – made almost entirely out of sugar.

Despite the long Anglo-Spanish war, London and Bristol were importing raw and refined sugar from plantations on Portuguese Madeira and the Spanish Azores and, after the defeat of the Armada in 1588, Bristol merchants were free to send their own ships and build sugar refineries. While sugar remained fabulously expensive, a luxuriously appointed banquet table boasted that no expense had been spared. This was the opportunity to impress and the banquet course alone could almost ruin an over-zealous host. The queen was known to have had a very sweet tooth – as a result of which in later life her teeth were black. (It is said that her ladies-in-waiting blackened their teeth to copy her, but it's more likely that their teeth were just as rotten as those of their queen.)

Several English cookery books in circulation at this time included recipes for 'ambrosial banquetting stuffes'. Gervase Markham gave this advice in *The English Hus-wife* (1615) for a banquet course (which started with the ubiquitous decorated March-paine or marchpane – marzipan – that always took pride of place):

> ... your preserved fruits shall be disht up first, your Pastes next, your wet Suckets after them, then, your dried Suckets [preserved fruit], then your Marmalades, and Cotiniades [fruits preserved in syrup], then your Comfrets of all kindes [comfits: sweets of spiced seeds in sugar], Next your Peares, Apples, Wardens, bak't, raw or rosted, and your Orenges and Lemmons sliced; and lastly your Wafer-cakes ... no two dishes of one kinde, going or standing together, and this will not only appear delicate to the eye, but invite the appetite with the much varietie thereof.

The names of many of the sweet dishes served as a banquet course may sound familiar to modern readers, but the Elizabethan version was often rather different.

Some Daintie Conceits

Marchpane or Marzipan

This has never gone out of favour and is still used to make sweets and to decorate cakes. It was made with ground almonds, sugar and rosewater beaten together with colouring and added spices such as cinnamon or clove. The strong, thick paste could then be worked into confections of all sorts of shapes and sizes and easily coloured; yellow with saffron and egg yolk; azurite blue; spinach for green; milk curds for white; and then also sometimes gilded with gold leaf. Some marzipan mixes contained pistachio, which gave a pale green colour. Once shaped, it was baked or dried in a cool oven on a base of wafers.

Marmalade

The modern idea of marmalade spread on toast for breakfast did not come along until well into the eighteenth century. Originally *chardequince*, a French word for a pulp made from quinces, it became *marmelada*, the Portuguese name for a sweet, solid quince paste imported in the late Middle Ages and mostly used by the very rich as a medicine. When lemons and bitter oranges began to arrive in Bristol, they were pulped with apples and sugar into stiff conserves. Other fruits, such as damsons, apples, pears and peaches, were also made into *marmalettes*. These were solid confections kept in small wooden boxes or moulded into fancy shapes, sometimes known as a 'brick of marmalade', which could be cut into slices and eaten with the fingers or a sucket fork as a banquet sweetmeat.

Gingerbread

Late medieval gingerbreads were made from a thick mixture of honey, ginger, spices such as cinnamon and pepper and breadcrumbs, sometimes coloured yellow with saffron or red with powdered sandalwood. This was stirred together, rolled thin and put to dry in a cool oven. Gingerbread was ornamented by impressing designs from elaborate and beautifully carved wooden moulds. Queen Elizabeth I had gingerbread figures made in the likeness of some of her important guests. By the eighteenth century, chopped preserved fruits, butter and eggs enriched the mixture and raising agents made it lighter and more like a cake that was baked in the oven. Spicy gingerbreads and cakes have remained popular and children still love to eat gingerbread men.

Suckets (Succade)

These sweetmeats were either 'wet suckets', which were fruits preserved in a thick syrup, or 'sucket candy', which were pieces of fruit steeped in sugar then dried. Candied fruit and nuts included: medlars, quinces, warden pears, peaches, sweet chestnuts, apricots, 'Damaske plumbes', cherries, grapes, filberts, almonds and figs. Candied and crystallised fruit and peel were rather similar to modern Western Christmas fare. Wet suckets were usually dished in glass bowls so that their fine colour and translucency could be shown off. Sucket candies were piled in smaller raised glasses. (The word candy, still used in the USA, is said to be derived from India, where sweet-making was an ancient art – the Sanskrit term, *khanda*, means sugar in pieces.)

Syllabubs, Junkets and Jellies

Cream was either whipped with a whisk made of hard white rushes until it was very thick or clotted over the fire, then cooled and strewn with sugar. Sherry and nutmeg might be stirred in to make 'sack cream'. A syllabub was a drink of separated wine and cream served in little glass syllabub pots with two handles and a spout which came out from the bottom. The clear, sweet, wine-rich whey would be drunk through this spout and then the creamy curd floating on top would be eaten with a spoon. Syllabub survived into the twentieth century as a more solid dessert but is now rarely made. Junket, now also out of fashion, was a dish of sweetened and flavoured curds produced by the action of rennet on milk – preferably still warm from the cow. Modern sweet fruit jellies, essential for children's parties, really only began to appear when pectin was discovered in the 1820s. Similarly, the modern sweet blancmange (French for 'white food'), made with milk and cornflour, was originally a savoury dish made of shredded chicken breast, sugar, rice and either ground almonds or almond milk.

Tartstuff and Custard

Fruit boiled in syrup and heavily flavoured with spices was used to make a thick fruit pulp known as *tartstuff*, which was often 'drawn up' with beaten eggs and thick cream to fill a sweet tart. Fruit pulp was also mixed with almonds, cream, sugar and eggs and used liberally in banquet dishes such as trifles, fools, white pots, boiled custards, syllabubs and junkets flavoured with sugar, cinnamon and nutmeg. Custards made with a mixture of milk and eggs and thickened by gentle heating were used as a filling in a range of flans and tarts (derived from the French *crustade*, a tart with a crust). Surprisingly, the modern pouring custard, now more often made from a packet, is much sweeter. Fruit creams, an early type of fruit fool made with eggs, cream and puréed fruit, were also

popular. Beaten white of eggs produced the favourite 'dishful of snow' – a spectacular centrepiece for the banquet course. Eggs were beaten with thick cream, rosewater and sugar until the froth rose, and then built up over an apple pulp with 'a thick bush of rosemary' on a platter. Sometimes the snow was gilded with gold dust as a final touch.

Comfits

These were small, coloured, hard and sugar-coated seeds or nuts, and there were also comfits of sugar-spun anise or other spices – all eaten as sweets or used to decorate other dishes. 'Kissing' comfits made with caraway seed were supposed to sweeten the breath. Multicoloured sugared almonds and gobstoppers are modern survivors of these comfits.

Wafers, Biscuits and Small Cakes

Biscuits of several different types joined the wafers which had formerly been served with hippocras wine to mark the end of the medieval meal. There were light, dry biscuits and biscuit-breads that used sugar, flour, a little honey and several spices bound with rosewater to make a biscuit paste that was cooked or dried in very cool ovens. Many of these came from Italy and were popular since they were thought 'to comfort the stomach and make a sweet breath'. There were also little almond macaroons and richer shortcakes made with butter, cream and well-beaten egg. These were often shaped into interlaced 'jumballs' or knots and sprinkled with sugar. The greatest innovation was the discovery that eggs could be used as a raising agent. A well-beaten egg served to raise an early form of sponge cake as well as macaroons and almond or saffron cakes.

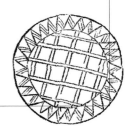

The banquet course was about amusement with 'Daintie conceits' – the cleverer and more inventive the better. A walnut cracked open revealed tiny 'Biskets and Carrawayes in it, or a pretty Poesey written'. Marchpane (marzipan) always appeared in some form or other at a banquet course: perhaps a wide dish filled with marzipan fruits like a still-life painting; delicately sculpted animals, trees and flowers; or spectacular models of sailing ships with cannon that fired. One particularly dramatic display was of a stag modelled from marzipan with an arrow sticking out of its side. When the senior lady guest was invited to pull out the arrow, sweet-spiced red wine flowed from the wound like blood and was caught by a server in a basin and later drunk by the guests. Queen Elizabeth, who loved to slice open a live stag's throat, must have particularly enjoyed this one.

Anything made of sugar was regarded as so desirable and so costly that sugar items could be accepted as bribes or gifts by the highest classes, and it was customary to give a distinguished visitor some sweetmeats, wine and sugar. Expensive boxes of marmalades decorated with coats of arms were often offered. But sugar-crazed royals and aristocrats could be extremely fussy and difficult. Henry VIII was said to have been pleased with his lavish gift of 'sweet goodys' from Bristol but not so Robert, Earl of Leicester, one of Queen Elizabeth's favourites and Bristol's new Lord High Steward. He proved to be a very ineffectual representative of the city's interests at court and several expensive gifts failed to improve things. When the earl and his brother, the Earl of Warwick, paid Bristol a visit in 1587, elaborate preparations were made to do them honour with five days of pageantry, feasting and hospitality. They finally rode off to Bath, taking with them six horse-loads of banqueting 'stuffe', which included 70 lb of loaf sugar, 40 lb of marmalade and suckets, a large barrel of conserves, 50 lb of raisins and 104 lb of figs. This staggering amount, however, failed to please the earl, who further demanded the gift of a new bed. The obsequious Corporation duly paid up for a 'feather bed with a cannapayne and curtains of green sail'. To the great relief of the city council the earl died the following year (it is said that he was poisoned), and the queen's Secretary, Lord Burghley, accepted the vacant position. When he accompanied the queen to Bristol, Burghley seemed very satisfied to receive his more modest gift of a gallon of claret, two gallons of sack, a large sugar loaf weighing 50 lb, two boxes of marmalade 'gilded very fair' and four barrels of suckets.

John Young gave the queen a jewel, in the form of a salamander and phoenix, and she rewarded him with a knighthood. Sir John completed his banqueting houses, possibly in anticipation of his queen returning to stay in his house, but he died in 1598. Elizabeth I did plan a second progress to Bristol in 1602, but it was cancelled due to bad weather and the queen's failing health. She died a year later in Richmond Palace, London.

THE WIDENING WORLD – NEW FOODS IN THE SIXTEENTH CENTURY

By the close of the sixteenth century, most of our present-day foodstuffs had already been introduced into England. Yet few of these new ingredients found immediate favour with cooks or appeared on dinner tables – in fact neither of today's staples, the potato and tomato, were overnight successes. Unusual and exotic-looking introductions were often received with suspicion and ignored for a long time. Partly due to health concerns and cost, it may also have been down to the typically British reluctance to eat anything new and foreign.

Conquistadors and explorers found all sorts of new foods in the course of exploring the New World, which they shipped home to show to their families and friends. On their voyages in the West Indies, explorers such as Columbus and Cortés are credited with discovering several kinds of foods previously unknown in Europe: turtle meat, sweet potatoes, capsicums (peppers), chilli peppers, plaintain and 'Jamaica pepper' (allspice). From Central and South America, explorers and colonists came back with the pineapple, 'Indian corn' or maize from Mexico, papaya, cacao beans, avocado, tomato, potato, soursop and beans (which the French called haricot). Many of these food discoveries were first taken to Spain, from where they travelled slowly north to England. The Portuguese introduced new citrus fruits such as sweet oranges from the Orient and bananas from the west coast of Africa. These novelties were probably sold to the captains of Bristol ships on regular visits to ports in Spain and Portugal but remained relatively unknown to most people for enturies to come.

One introduction that did find immediate favour was the turkey. A native of Mexico and Central America, these birds were discovered in the 1520s by Hernán Cortés on his expedition to conquer New Spain. The turkey acquired its name after being confused with guinea fowl coming from Africa and sold by 'turkey merchants', meaning Turks. The large, sweet-fleshed turkey was quickly preferred to stringy great birds such as the swan, heron and crane, and domesticated turkeys were soon available in the markets and regularly appeared at big feasts and holidays. At first they were fabulously expensive, but by mid century could be bought in Bristol markets for five shillings apiece. The West Indian green sea turtle was another instant hit. After Columbus' men discovered that live turtles weighing up to 100 lb could survive transportation to Europe in ships' water tanks, turtle meat became a fashionable delicacy: roast turtle, turtle pies or the ubiquitous turtle soup were essential dinner-party dishes until well into the nineteenth century.

Despite their natural sweetness, sweet potatoes were slow to gain popularity. In 1589, the Bristol historian, John Hakluyt, described sweet potatoes as 'the most delicate roots that may be eaten; and doe farre exceed our passeneps [parsnips] or carets [carrots]'. But English cooks were not clear how to cook and eat them and comfit makers insisted on candying them for eating as banqueting delicacies. In his 1597 *Herball or General Historie of Plantes*, the English botanist, John Gerard, described how sweet potato was eaten roasted and infused with wine, boiled with prunes or roasted with oil, vinegar and salt. He also suggested that it 'comforts, strengthens, and nourishes the body', as well as 'procuring bodily lust'. Its reputation as an aphrodisiac could be the reason for the popularity of sweet potatoes in Tudor England. Henry VIII consumed massive amounts of them – especially spiced sweet potato pie – and Shakespeare's Falstaff exclaims in *The Merry of Wives of Windsor* (1602): 'Let the sky rain potatoes; let it thunder to the tune of Green Sleeves, hail kissing-comfits and snow eringoes'. (Eryngo, or sea holly, was also thought to have aphrodisiac qualities; its roots were candied and used to sweeten the breath – hence the mention of 'kissing-comfits'.)

The white potato, which arrived in Europe later in the century, was often confused with sweet potatoes. John Gerard mistakenly called white potatoes 'Virgin potatoes' because they had first been shipped to Britain from Virginia, New England. But their origins lay in Peru and Chile, where hundreds of different varieties of potato are still cultivated. Again, cooks were unsure how to treat them. Gerard wrote that he roasted them in embers, or boiled and ate them with oil, vinegar and pepper or added them to pies mixed with sugar and fruits. There is a legend that when Sir Walter Raleigh introduced the potato to Queen Elizabeth I, she complained 'not enough salt', and certainly the potato failed to become popular until the late eighteenth century. But when it was discovered that white potatoes could be very easily cultivated, they became the staple crop in Ireland and England and gradually replaced the basic starches in poor men's diet of dried peas, lentils and beans.

When the 'tomata', or apple of love, arrived from Mexico via Spain in the 1570s it was considered 'devoid of nourishment and chill to the stomach' and also thought capable of causing gout or cancer. Gerard described tomatoes as having a 'rank and stinking savour' but thought they might be grown as an attractive ornamental plant, and so the tomato was banished to the garden, where it was cultivated as an ornamental with decorative fruits. The aubergine was similarly ignored and thought 'very dangerous and hurtful'.

As for vegetables, cauliflowers arrived in Bristol from Sicily; garden rhubarb, considered a good laxative, from Italy; there was red Russian cabbage and Spanish lettuce. When Catherine of Aragon was a young queen in England, in the early 1500s, salad greens were so rare that she had to send to Holland for lettuce and herbs. Fortunately, Flemish Protestant refugees, skilled gardeners who cultivated all kinds of vegetables and fruit, started settling along the east coast of Britain in the later 1500s and brought seeds of their better strains of plants, such as the orange carrot, globe artichokes, asparagus, cardoons and cucumbers. Vegetable gardens, even in town, were suddenly very popular and fresh garden produce certainly improved the diet of the better off. Chicory, endive, mallow, fennel and rocket became popular salad plants grown in the kitchen garden.

Looking forward to the years after Elizabeth's reign, coffee, tea and chocolate had arrived in England virtually simultaneously by the mid 1600s, although they originated in three different continents – Africa, Asia and America respectively – and came by different routes. Coffee had long been known in the Middle East when, around 1615, Venetian merchants introduced the drink to Europe; by the 1650s, coffee houses were becoming popular meeting places, especially in London, Oxford and Bristol. Tea was brought from China by Dutch East India Company merchants and was first sold in Amsterdam, in 1610, for a staggering £10 per lb. The price dropped after Britain's own East India Company began to ship home supplies, although high customs duties meant tea smuggling was carried out on a large scale, including by Bristol. Tea arrived properly in England in 1657, but as a luxury drink. As for chocolate, by 1647 it was being advertised in English newspapers for its medicinal qualities: an 'excellent West Indian drink called Chocolate … it cures and preserves the body of many diseases'. When Cromwell's forces took Jamaica from the Spaniards in 1655, cacao plantations were already flourishing there and the island became England's main source for chocolate. Like coffee and tea, chocolate was believed to be a powerful aphrodisiac. Consumers also appreciated the stimulant effects of caffeine in these drinks (chocolate as a drink contains a small amount of caffeine), which, unlike alcohol, did not make them drunk.

After London, Bristol in the 1500s and 1600s was the next most major port of call for ships with cargos of food luxuries, and Bristol women could count themselves lucky to be first in line for new arrivals at the docks. Shopkeepers, keeping careful watch on records of ships tying up on the quays, would make sure of stocking up before goods were sent to inland markets. Better-class shops now sold fancy food items such as Spanish oils, common spices including cumin, coriander, mace, pepper and ginger, comfits and sweetmeats, Flemish treacle, marmalades and dried fruits such as dates, prunes and raisins. Other foods from abroad included vermicelli, macaroni and Parmesan cheese from Italy; Dutch cheeses; olives from Greece and capers from France; a relish made of grey mullet or tuna roes, called *botargo*, came from the Mediterranean. Other foods arrived with travellers returning from lands as distant as Persia, India and China. Gradually, all the many new kinds of foods found their way, from near and far, into English – and Bristolian – kitchens and began to alter the nation's and city's tastes and transform their meals.

WAR AND PEACE

BRISTOL UNDER SIEGE – THE ENGLISH CIVIL WAR

Dawn was beginning to break on 10 September 1645 as Parliamentary troops retook the city of Bristol from Royalist forces. High up on the parapet of the battery on Prior's Hill Fort, Kingsdown, Oliver Cromwell and his General, Sir Thomas Fairfax, looked out over the city and watched as fires, started by the occupying Royalists, took hold: 'the town was fired in three places by the enemy, which we could not put out; and this began a great trouble to the General and us all, fearing to see so famous a city burnt to ashes before our faces', Cromwell recalled. Fortunately, a few hours later, Prince Rupert, the Royalist commander, surrendered and brought to an end the second attack suffered by the people of Bristol during the English Civil War. Later that day, as Cromwell's soldiers entered Bristol, an observer described the terrible state the city had been reduced to:

> It looked more like a prison than a city, and the people more like prisoners than citizens; being brought so low with taxations, so poor in habits, and so dejected in countenance; the streets so noisome, and the houses so nasty as they were unfit to receive friends till they were cleansed.

Buffeted first by one side and then the other, Bristol had been dragged reluctantly into a conflict which it did not want and which it had done its best to avoid. Bristolians were not concerned with national issues of religion and politics and no one wanted a war – it was bad for business. Under pressure from both sides to commit, the Common Council remained stubbornly neutral and never declared for either King or Parliament. Fearful of attack, it ordered workmen to strengthen walls and forts and add 16 guns to the castle armoury. The women were left to fend for themselves and their families and protect their homes and store-cupboards. Faced with the possibility of a long siege, they bought up all the groceries they could find in the market and scoured the surrounding countryside for wild food. They set about salting, drying and preserving, and then hiding their food reserves. Barrels of butter, sacks of flour, honey pots, sugar loaves, pots of conserves, preserves and pickles, whole cheeses, hogsheads of ale and flagons of wine were taken down to their cellars. The most precious spices and sugar were locked away in secret places, sides of bacon were hung high out of sight in the chimney and dried fruit and hard bread was tied in canvas bags and hidden under the floorboards.

The Council was still playing for time when Parliamentary troops arrived at the city gates on 9 December 1642. Desperate to avoid bloodshed or even starvation by siege, the mayor's wife and a hundred other 'prominent' women marched on the Council, demanding the gates be opened so that 'parliaments forces might in a faire and peaceable manner be admitted'. They may later have regretted their action when they discovered that having an army billeted on them was unpleasant and expensive. The Council sent a petition to the king in London asking him to be reconciled with Parliament and to end hostilities so that business could return to normal: 'Our ships lie now rotting in the Harbor without any Mariners freight or trade unto forraigne partes by reason of our home-bred distraction ....' But Cromwell's soldiers continued to eat all the food carefully hoarded by the townswomen and the war went on.

In March 1643, a plot among some aggrieved Puritan citizens to let Royalist troops into the city was quickly foiled and the ringleaders were hanged in Wine Street, leaving two widows and sixteen children. Meanwhile, the occupying troops raised a line of earthwork defences and forts around the north-west of the city – from Brandon Hill Fort and Windmill Hill Fort (now Royal Fort) to Prior's Hill Fort on Kingsdown – in readiness for an attack or a long siege. But, in July, Prince Rupert and the king's men attacked, and for several days the two armies kept up heavy fire, with many casualties on both sides. There is a story that about 200 ladies, led by a Puritan, Mrs Dorothy Hazzard, rushed to the Frome Gate with sledge-loads of woolsacks, which they used to block the gate which guarded the bridge over the river Frome. They also brought food for the soldiers and urged them to stand firm, assuring them that they would face the besiegers themselves, with their children in their arms, 'to keep off the shot from the soldiers if they were afraid'. But the Royalists took the city anyway, the Parliamentary troops fled and Bristol was left with a new and even less agreeable occupying force.

After their swift victory, the Royalist army held Bristol for over two years. A large garrison of soldiers was billeted in the city, 20–30 men to a house, forcing householders to be turned out of their beds and stripping them of all their food, furniture, bedding and kitchen things. Bands of violent, drunken soldiers made daily threats to people's life and property and looted shops and bonded warehouses full of the finest imported wines, spices, dried fruits and

Widow Kelly and other women barricading the Frome Gate against the Royalists at the Siege of Bristol, 1643.
From Nicholls & Taylor, 1881

sugar. All that remained of the food supplies hidden by housewives was found and consumed and their husband's cellars emptied. Already faced with huge extra taxation and loss of foreign and domestic trade, on which it depended for its wealth, the city was fined further for supporting Parliament and allowing its troops in. The sufferings were made even worse when a bout of plague killed around 3,000 people. On the plus side, the king, anxious to build up Bristol as an important and strategic city, granted a charter to the Society of Merchant Venturers which opened new trade routes to Russia and the Levant. He also ordered the establishment of a royal mint and the setting up of a printing press.

But these welcome opportunities were short-lived. In other parts of the country, the tide was turning against the king. In September 1645, when it became clear that the fall of Bristol would finish the king, Cromwell headed west with his forces, taking Bridgwater then Bath and the fort at Portishead where Parliamentary warships blockaded the Avon and land forces went on to surround the city. On 10 September, at one o'clock in the morning, Cromwell gave the signal to retake Bristol.

After the war, Cromwell ordered the destruction of several English and Welsh castles including Bristol's, which was then described as 'a large, old castle, but weake'. Despite strengthening and repairs, it was no match for modern cannon fire and its grounds had become a refuge for the homeless and beggars, thieves and highwaymen. It took more than a year to reduce it to a quarry supplying stone for the rebuilding of the city, ravaged by civil war. The great Norman castle, which had always stood apart and aloof from the city, was no more.

BACK TO BUSINESS

Three years after the Restoration of the monarchy in 1660, King Charles II visited Bristol and was hailed with delight by citizens tired of the restrictions and religious oppression imposed on them by the Puritans. A tremendous and costly banquet was given for the king at the Great House. Nine cooks were hired to dress the food and the royal party did particular justice to the famous Spanish sherry; a sweet white wine which in those days was known as sack. The city began to recover from the war, with new houses going up and streets pushing beyond the old city boundary walls, creating pleasant suburbs for the wealthy classes. Life was looking up for Bristol; it was back to business.

The puritanical Commonwealth government had denied people innocent amusements such as the maypole, the Christmas feast, the Sunday walk and other pleasures – people now wanted to relax and have fun. The Church and Bristol Council made sure that their perambulation of the city boundaries, a custom that had been suspended for several years, was restored with traditional entertainments and presents of cheese, cakes, marmalade, conserves, comfits, caraways, fruit and beer distributed to the people. On Boxing Day, the 'Horn Fair' was held in Wade Street, taking its name from a grotesque-looking ginger-bread cake known as 'the horn', which was made to represent a man's head and shoulders, with two trumpets branching from its back; they varied in size from a few inches to a yard long. A local news-sheet described how 'From morning till night groups of pleasure-seekers wandered up and down amongst the stalls selling hundreds of "gilt horns" and other sweetmeats, staking their pence until their pockets were emptied.' A similar fair was held on New Year's Day in West Street. On Twelfth Night, the ancient custom of wassailing took place in the city orchards. The cider apple trees were woken from their winter sleep and wassailed, an Anglo-Saxon word meaning 'good health', to ensure a good crop for the following autumn. The roots of the oldest tree were anointed with cider and, after the Apple Queen was crowned, she placed a piece of toast in the branches for the wren and the robin. Old wassailing songs were sung by Morris dancers and guns fired into the trees to drive away evil spirits, whilst everyone warmed themselves around a blazing bonfire and consumed hot punch and gingerbread.

The Marsh was reclaimed and used as a recreation area with a bowling green 'for Merchants and Gentlemen' and a promenade with avenues of trees and meadows – 'Here, too, the student wanders meditating the arts, and the happy lover walks with his darling.' Charles II was a keen seaman and he introduced yacht racing from Holland, where he had spent his exile. Bristol took up the craze and yachting competitions were held on the Avon and Frome. Fishing and swimming contests, archery and wrestling matches drew large crowds of spectators. Other public entertainments included a new ducking stool for women 'scolds' and stocks for minor felons.

The city's wine trade had been badly hit when Cromwell passed an act embargoing Dutch trading ships, which had carried much of the French wines to Bristol. Until the prohibition was relaxed, merchants turned once again to dealing in sweet wines and sherry from Portugal and Madeira. Visitors to Bristol's waterfront often noted the curious use of dog-sledges rather than horse-drawn carts. As an anonymous writer noted in *A New Present State of England*:

> No carts being permitted to come there, lest as some say, the Shake occasion'd by them on the Pavement should affect their Bristol Milk, a Cant term for their sherry in the vaults, large quantities whereof are doubtless stored there and dispos'd of both wholesale and retail in its utmost Purity and Perfection.

A vast underground world of cellars spread slowly, deep beneath the city streets. Here the precious wines and sherries were stored and matured in undisturbed and secure conditions. People also drank more home-brewed ale, and books of instruction began to appear on how to make wine and cider from home-grown fruits. Increasing demand for sugar meant that several more sugar refineries were built to process imports of raw sugar loaf from the new colonies.

Bristol's postwar recovery and growth was attracting tourists, who took advantage of easier travel to come and enjoy the city's attractions. The first public coach from London to Bristol was established; under good conditions the journey took three long days, travelling 'from dawn to dusk'. In June 1654, the 'genial and cultivated diarist', John Evelyn, paid a visit to Bristol. He compared the city favourably with London: 'Not for its large extent, but manner of building, shops, bridge, traffic, exchange, market place etc.' Sugar and wine, especially sherry, were the major businesses and merchants were eager to show off their new sugar refineries and well-stocked cellars to important visitors. Evelyn was invited to a sugar house, where he first saw 'the

THE
LAMENTABLE
COMPLAINTS
OF
NICK FROTH the Tapfter, and
RVLEROST the Cooke.

Concerning the reftraint lately fet forth,
againft drinking, potting, and piping on the Sab-
bath day, and againft felling meate.

A broadside of 1641. The tapster and cook complain of regulations preventing them from trading on Sundays. A proclamation from Bristol's *Little Red Book* stated that: 'No taverner of wine or ale may keep any guests sitting in their taverns after the hour of curfew has rung under the penalty of 2s'.
Peter Brears

manner of sugar refining and casting it into loaves'. He enjoyed 'a collation of eggs fried in the sugar furnace, washed down with excellent Spanish wine, celebrated over the whole kingdom as Bristol Milk'.

In 1668, Evelyn's friend, the diarist Samuel Pepys (clerk to the Navy Board), visited Bristol, with his wife Eliza and her Bristol-born maid, Deb Willet. On arrival, they stopped at the Horse Shoe, an inn on Wine Street where 'a handsome fellow' trimmed his hair. The party moved on to The Sun in Christmas Street, where Pepys left his wife and strolled off to explore the quay and inspect the Custom House and the dry dock, where a new warship was being built for the Royal Navy. Like Evelyn, Pepys described Bristol as 'another London … the second greatest city of the kingdom with so many houses that one could not see the fields'. He was struck by the splendour of the city and its wealthiest citizens, who instead of riding in gilded carriages, walked the streets with trains of servants in rich liveries and kept tables loaded with good cheer. Pepys was also curious to see 'carts without wheels or horses' carrying goods drawn on sledges by dogs, and was told that this was to prevent a

The Llandoger Tavern. Drawing by Samuel Loxton from an early engraving.
Courtesy of the Bristol City Reference Library

rumbling of carts' wheels over the cobbles that might disturb the cellars beneath, with their stores of 'that golden velvet wine which lay in the vaults below'. A special feature of their visit was the hospitality of Deb's uncle. Pepys recalled a good dinner and 'a fine entertainment from this noble merchant, of strawberries and venison pasty and abundance of brave wine and, above all, Bristol milk'.

Bristol taverns mostly sold wine and advertised themselves with branches and leaves hung over the door. The Green Lattis (later called the Rummer) in High Street was believed to have been the first to open, as early as 1241. Such taverns were kept by vintners, who had a virtual monopoly on the retail wine trade. One disgruntled pilgrim complained that ale houses were convivial drinking establishments mostly found down on the quays, where they served seamen and workers who drank from earthenware or pewter pots, talked and sang, gambled and even enjoyed the services of a prostitute. Heavy drinking was a national pastime and any feast or festivity meant an excuse for a drunken orgy. Ale was mostly brewed by the 'ale-wife', who often hawked it about in the market place. It was usually thin and sour and went off quickly.

While ale houses and taverns lining the quays supplied refreshment and entertainment for mariners, smart new coaching inns were opening their doors 'for respectable visitors' in the more salubrious parts of town. The most popular names for Bristol inns had marine connections, such as The Ship Inn or the Three Mariners and the still-famous Llandoger Trow in King Street. When

Captain Hawkins retired from the sea in 1664, he opened an inn called Llandogo on King Street behind Welsh Back, an area frequented by seafarers. For some reason the name was later changed to Llandoger Trow – a trow being a flat-bottomed barge. The inn was a regular recruiting place for privateer ships. One Bristol newspaper published an advertisement:

> *The Tyger*, a privateer, for a four month cruise. All officers, seamen, landsmen and others that are willing to enter on board the said privateer, let them repair to the Sign of the Llandogar Trow in King Street, where they will meet with proper encouragement.

Sea trade was always riven with ferocious smuggling, piracy and privateering, and even whilst holding high office such as mayor or alderman, Bristol merchants were deeply involved in all three. Privateers were really just pirates given permission during wartime to attack and seize enemy ships and their goods for the State. Privateers, pirates and press gangs daily crammed the bars of the inns and taverns and roamed the streets, pouncing on experienced keelmen and any young man who might make a sailor. Even factory workers were taken and business suffered.

It is popularly believed that the Bristol-born pirate, Captain Bluebeard, frequented the Llandoger Trow. Other stories that continue to haunt the old inn, which is still serving customers, include one that it was here that Robert Louis Stevenson found inspiration for the character of Admiral Benbow in *Treasure Island*. According to another tradition, this is where Daniel Defoe met Alexander Selkirk, whose adventures inspired the great classic, *Robinson Crusoe*. Like many of Bristol's enduring tales, these are mostly the stuff of legend and romance, though none the worse for it – they imbue Bristol's character with a salty, maritime, adventuring spirit and make a vibrant contrast to the somewhat duller business side of the city.

Three years later, Pepys returned to Bristol on navy business, to inspect the royal forests and timber for the king's ships, as the fleet was preparing for a major confrontation with the Dutch. He travelled in a lumbering coach and four with three other officials – 'their bewigged faces peering out and four clerks riding beside them'. When they reached Bristol, they put up in an inn for two days. Respectable inns provided travellers with both lodging and food, and although guests often had to share beds with each other, along with bedbugs, the fare was reasonably wholesome and cheap. The menu might include cuts of cold meats such as chine of beef, veal or neat's (veal) tongue, mutton chops, hams and pies with local cheeses, cheap oysters, sturgeon or lobster, followed by gooseberry tart washed down with beer, cider or wine.

Pepys and his companions' bill in Bristol came to £5 8s 9d, plus six shillings more for servants, six for claret and another six for the waterman, three-and-six for a trip down the river and half-a-crown for having their linen washed. They took the ferry across the Severn to Wales to visit the iron works at Chepstow and stayed at an inn where they enjoyed a dinner of a leg of mutton with carrots, a couple of rabbits, fruit and cheese, a bottle of claret, a pint of white wine, and bread and beer. The following night they ate a leg of mutton and cauliflowers, a breast of veal, six chickens, artichokes, peas, oranges, fruit and cheese and a 'modest' three-and-sixpence worth of wine. Pepys' detailed accounts of his eating seem generally to have been favourable, but his report on the timber in the Forest of Dean was not good. Half the oaks were 'wind-ridden or cup-shaken' and few were good for shipbuilding. Many of the best had already been felled for building a new warship at Bristol.

COFFEE, TEA AND CHOCOLATE

In 1652, the first coffee house opened in London. Its Greek owner claimed that coffee had medicinal qualities; it aided digestion, cured headaches, coughs, consumption, dropsy, gout and scurvy and kept people alert and awake, making one 'fit for business'. Soon there were hundreds of London houses and the fashion quickly spread to all the large cities, including Bristol. Pepys was a keen frequenter of the fashionable new coffee houses in London and on his second visit to Bristol may well have visited the city's first establishment. Coffee houses attracted politicians, artists, businessmen and the intelligentsia, who could pay a penny to drink a bowl of coffee, read the papers and indulge in stimulating conversation. 'You have all Manner of News there: You have a good Fire, which you may sit by as long as you please: You have a Dish of Coffee; you meet your Friends for the Transaction of Business, and all for a Penny, if you don't care to spend more.' Women were not permitted.

The first Bristol coffee house, called The Elephant, was in All Saints Lane. Others followed and soon rivalled taverns as places to meet. Particularly popular was The British Coffee House in Broad Street, where passengers from stagecoaches could stop for a reviving drink. On either side of the front entrance of the Exchange Building in Corn Street were a coffee house and a tavern, where important meetings took place. The coffee houses attracted city men who discussed shipping news and gossiped about local business and politics. Shipbuilders talked to shipowners, manufacturers to merchants, lawyers to financers. They would study the notices of sailings and auctions and read the latest political and foreign news; there was much divided opinion and argument about the war between Britain and her American colonies (there were many Bristolians who supported the conflict). Coffee houses were regarded with some suspicion by the authorities, who thought of them as hotbeds of dissent and trouble. It was alleged they were 'constantly frequented by seditious sectaries and disloyal persons, where visitors were entertained with false news, scandalous libels, and pamphlets dishonouring the Church and Government'. In 1681, Bristol Council recommended that 'no news, printed or written, and no pamphlet, should be suffered to be read in any coffee-house, unless it had been first sanctioned by the Mayor, or the Alderman of the Ward'. However, the authorities could not deny that, before the arrival of coffee, the English used to drink large daily amounts of alcohol. 'Nowadays,' one observer wrote, 'men sat together and drank a more sobering cup of coffee; for whereas Apprentices and Clerks with others, used to take their mornings' draught in Ale, Beer, or Wine, which by the dizziness they cause in the Brain, make many unfit for business, they use now to play the Goodfellows in the wakeful and civill drink.'

But not all Bristol's coffee houses were civilised or improving places. Many were described as noisy, chaotic, smelly and dirty and devoted to male company and male interests: 'There was a rabble going hither and thither; reminding me of a swarm of rats in a ruinous cheese', wrote one visitor, '… Some were scribbling, others were talking, some were drinking, some smoking, and some arguing; the whole place stank of tobacco like the cabin of a barge.' As far as the women were concerned, coffee houses were almost as pernicious places as a tavern or ale house. They complained, 'Why do our men Trifle away their time, scald their chops, and spend their Money, all for a little base, black, thick, nasty bitter stinking, nauseous Puddlewater?' In 1674, a group of women got up a Petition Against Coffee and published a pamphlet complaining that their menfolk spent the morning in a tavern 'til every one of them is as Drunk as a Drum, and then back again to the Coffeehouse to drink themselves sober'. Furthermore, the ladies claimed, coffee made men impotent: 'It has so *Eunucht* our Husbands, and *Crippled* our more kind gallants … they come from it with nothing more moist but their snotty Noses; nothing *Stiffe* in their Joints, nor *standing* but their Ears.' The male riposte was that, on the contrary, 'coffee makes erections more Vigorous, the Ejaculations more full, adds a spiritualescency to the Sperme'.

Fortunately, chocolate and tea became available around the same time as coffee, and the ladies were determined to make them their own. The drinking of these beverages could be done privately at home, in the bosom of the family, or as a polite social occasion. Chocolate and tea became increasingly popular among the wealthy, and afternoon tea was soon part of the fashionable social round. The mistress of the house would preside at the tea table and show off her delicate porcelain cups without handles and elegant silver teapots or chocolatiers. So many new, specially made cups, pots, kettles and urns were required that it stimulated Bristol's pottery and metalwork industries. There was also an increase in orders for sugar to sweeten these drinks, which were bitter-tasting. Tea, which was first drunk in the Chinese fashion as a weak infusion without milk, was so expensive that it was kept locked in the tea caddy and the key was kept by the lady of the house. Chocolate was bought in a cake or roll and had to be grated into hot liquid (at first wine or water and later milk) and then vigorously swizzled with a long, ridged stick called a *molinet*, until the cocoa and liquid had emulsified. It was then sweetened with sugar and flavoured with cinnamon, nutmeg or vanilla. Chocolate was also popular as a breakfast drink with added egg yolk, or as a bedtime nightcap fortified with Madeira wine or Bristol Milk.

Tearooms would soon begin to find favour among ladies requiring somewhere respectable to meet in town. In imitation of coffee shops for men, Thomas Twining opened the first 'Tea Shop for Ladies' in London in 1717. Soon after, a tea garden was opened in the old Vauxhall Gardens and the fashion quickly spread to large provincial cities. The New Vauxhall Pleasure Gardens in Bristol were built on the slopes between Dowry Square and the river and offered entertainments such as fireworks and concerts and a tea garden lit with lanterns in the trees. Coffee houses gradually declined and eventually many were turned into private men's clubs (in Bristol the Commercial Rooms and the Clifton Club) or chop houses.

GOING TO MARKET
Country gentry, who still provided most of their own food from their estates, remained largely unaware of the changing scene, content with old eating habits. But gradually they too were sending out for ingredients from the towns. Their household accounts reveal orders for surprising quantities of luxury food and drink ordered from town. When some West Country ladies visited Bristol on a shopping trip in 1692, their lists included: spices, sugar comfits, Genoa olives, fruit conserves, fine Italian cheeses as well as good Cheddar cheese, and cured salmon and oatcakes brought from Scotland. Sugar was becoming cheaper and so more could be purchased to make sweet puddings, preserves and sweetmeats. If you had money in your purse you could now buy an interesting choice of ingredients to put on the dinner table, and increasingly the shops and markets stocked a wider range of better-quality foodstuffs. Bristol's culinary life was centred on its market days and two annual fairs, which were among the largest in the country. The markets were described as follows by a local historian of the time:

Shops and stalls on the south side of Wine Street in the seventeenth century. Drawing by Samuel Loxton. Courtesy of Bristol City Reference Library

> Butter remarkable good and flesh meat, ox beef, veel and mutton, the best of every kind, together with all the produce of the kitchen-garden in great abundance, are to be had at the markets, held every Wednesday and Saturday, behind the Exchange in Union-Street.

Twice a week, fresh salmon, cod, mackerel, herring, plaice, flounders, oysters and sprats were unloaded on the Back to be sold at the fish market in Union Street. A prosperous Welsh fishmonger called Thomas Llewellyn and his son, a butter dealer, did brisk business 'during the Fish and Butter Season'; they also sold 'fine pickled Tenby oysters and sturgeon'. Welsh tradesmen supplied much of Bristol's food and had long been well established on Welsh Back, where trows from Wales unloaded their cargos and held a market every other Wednesday

> where the Welch boats, arriving at spring tides, discharged the produce of their country for sale; fine salt-butter, poultry of all kinds, roasting pigs and geese ready for the spit; fruit as apples and pears, etc.

Some Welsh drovers sailed their black cattle on small boats across the Severn before driving them into Bristol's cattle market. The great market for fat and lean cattle, and sheep, was held in St Thomas Street every Thursday and was 'much frequented by the woollen manufacturers at the season of the year for the purchase of wool, the Wool-Hall being in this street'. Farmers from all over the country could now bring in their produce to sell at market, after paying a fee, but were forbidden to hawk meat, bacon, butter or cheese from door to door. Any infringement of regulations over food sales was just as severely punished as it had been back in the Middle Ages – a baker called 'Peaceable' Robert Mathews was fined six guineas by the Bakers' Company for selling underweight bread.

Better transport meant regional specialities were also becoming more available: Newcastle salted haddock, Scotch salmon and Cheshire and Stilton cheeses were now widely known. More food from abroad turned up in the shops, too, such as sago from Malaya, vermicelli, macaroni and Parmesan cheese from Italy, piccalilli, curry, pilau rice from India and ketchups from China and Malaya. Wider travel also meant that tourists and traders were returning home with stories of wonderful foreign dishes and fresh tastes. One merchant, home from a trip to Verona, ordered his cook to produce Italian pasta and Parma ham. His wife served it to their guests, who loved the strange-tasting new dish and sent to town for pasta and ham in order to try it for themselves. The merchant may even have amazed his guests with descriptions of the Italian fork, which would soon come into common use in England, though for now the spoon, knife and hands remained the norm, even for refined tables.

Although it would still be many years before women were to play any significant role in Bristol public life, their influence and contribution in the home, particularly in the kitchen, increased considerably. The world was slowly changing around the town housewife's home and for her cook in the kitchen. People were becoming more interested in eating and talking about food. For the literate lady, several cookery books were available, such as *The Accomplisht Cook* (1660) by Robert May, the Mrs Beeton of his time, with its vast compendium of recipes and household advice, and *The Closet of the Eminently Learned Sir Kenelm Digby Kt, Open'd* (1677). All those strange new foods that had been coming into Bristol and London docks over the century suddenly seemed more attractive and were viewed with less suspicion than before. Inevitably, these early changes took place among the gentry class. They lent cookery books to each other, exchanged food plants to grow in their kitchen gardens and served exciting new dishes at their tables; their guests went home to tell their own friends and neighbours, and the word spread. People seemed to be doing all kinds of novel things with their food; some were sprinkling olive oil on their salad or using large amounts of butter for cooking or to dress vegeta-

A seventeenth-century family meal.
Peter Brears

bles. Cooks began to make pastry with eggs instead of just butter, making it richer and lighter. The once-fashionable French recipes were gradually becoming more English and housewives wanted less advice from grand men on kitchen matters.

The town housewife planned the meals, did most of the shopping and, depending on her wealth and status, either instructed a female cook or did the cooking herself with the assistance of a kitchen maid. She carried out all the seasonal business of preserving and distilling. She salted meat, preserved fruit, made quince jelly and damson jam and dried flowers for pot pourri. She prepared syrups and candied sweetmeats, distilled cordials and made up cosmetics and herbal remedies for the medicine cupboard. Gardens became a valuable source of fresh vegetables and herbs, and townswomen took a new interest in their bit of back garden. Up to now, women had learned by watching and listening and kept to traditional methods and unchanging menus. But old ingrained attitudes were undergoing a gradual transformation and even the most conservative town housewife was beginning to wake up to culinary changes in her kitchen as well as the opportunity to have some creative control there. Dozens of more modern household and cookery books began to appear in response to this growing interest.

England's first printed cookbook was sold in 1500, followed by a flood of little manuals directed increasingly at the housewife and her staff: *The Good Huswifes Jewell, The Good Hous-Wives Treasurie, The Good Huswives Closet and The Good Huswives Handmaid. The English Huswife* by Gervase Markham, which first appeared in 1615, was so influential it continued to be reprinted until the end of the century. Markham was concerned with his reader's personality and ability as mother and homemaker: 'Our English housewife', he wrote,

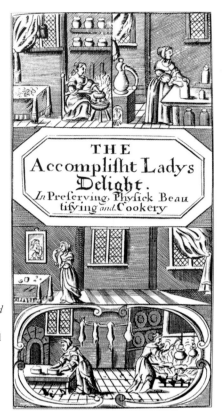

The title page for Hannah Woolley's *Accomplished Lady's Delight* (sixth edition, 1684) which depicts the housewife cooking, preserving, distilling and preparing medicines and cosmetics.

must be of chaste thoughts, stout courage, patient, untyred, watchfull, diligent, witty, pleasant, constant in friendship, full of good Neighbor-Hood, wise in discourse but not frequent therein – sharp and quick of speech but not bitter or talkative, secret in her affaires, comfortable in her counsels, and generally skilfull in the worthy knowledges which do belong to her vocation.

But she was also expected to know her business in the kitchen: 'To speak then of the outward and active knowledges which belong unto our English House-wife, I hold the first and most principal to be, a perfect knowledge and skill in cookery.' Markham was a stickler for quality and he made a great point of presenting enticing dishes and encouraged the housewife to 'invite the appetite with variety.'

But this was not a time of good living for everyone. Several serious harvest failures and food shortages were compounded by the terrible suffering and disruption during the Civil War. They were described as 'probably the most terrible years of food scarcity through which the country had ever passed'. For the majority of the population, hunger was a very real experience.

GEORGIAN BRISTOL
Putting on London Airs

FOOD REBELLION

On 21 May 1709, 200 colliers from the Bristol Kingswood mines marched into the city armed with cudgels and raised a riot. They were joined by other hungry, angry workers; sufficient to frighten the authorities into promising to reduce the price of corn. A succession of poor harvests and hard winters, along with war with France during the early 1700s, had pushed up the price of food alarmingly, while the rapid decline of Bristol's cloth industry increased the numbers of the poor. A bushel of corn had doubled in price, putting basic bread almost beyond the reach of the poorest citizens. When the Council ordered Bristol bakers to lower their prices, their response was to 'shutt up their ovens', but they were compelled to submit when the magistrates broke with normal restrictive practices and threatened to allow country bakers to sell their bread in the city. Food riots were the staple of eighteenth-century agitation among the poor. If grain was insufficient or its price too high, the poor could either go hungry or riot. It brought their plight to the attention of the authorities, who sometimes responded positively but on other occasions with violence.

Bristol continued to be run by the virtually self-appointed band of councillors and aldermen that usually comprised city merchants and that had the mayor and sheriff at its helm. Among them were the powerful Bristol aristocrats, the Merchant Venturers – the ancient trading association which held the purse strings and the votes for any change. But the extravagance and power of the city fathers was beginning to be questioned. As the price of most food continued to be far too high, there were more violent disturbances in Bristol and other towns, which led to the creation of the famous Riot Act of 1715. If there was any kind of gathering or disturbance, an official such as the mayor or sheriff would 'read the Riot Act', ordering the dispersal within the hour of any group of more than 12 people who were 'unlawfully, riotously, and tumultuously assembled together' on pain of facing severe punishment, including death. But the people of Bristol were not cowed by this. Unrest continued, especially among the more vocal and organised colliers and weavers who lived and worked on city's margins. Violent mobs began rioting against all kinds of grievances; against the king, unemployment, toll gates and the high price of food, which resulted in several deaths. 'We might as well be hanged as starved to death' was the popular cry.

This was also a time of rapid population growth. Back in 1700, the population within the old city walls was at bursting point and within only 50 years it had doubled. Yet living conditions had changed little since the Middle Ages. People were packed into ancient timber and plaster houses with roofs overhanging congested narrow streets and an open drain down the centre in which pigs foraged. The Avon and Frome rivers acted as open sewers and the water supply, once the pride of the town, had collapsed. Not surprisingly there were numerous outbreaks of plague, cholera and typhoid and other diseases were rife. The air was thick with the fumes of coal smoke from home fires and factory furnaces, with poisonous chemicals from dye works and bleaching houses. The stench of tanneries, town drains, filthy rivers, garbage and rotting food must have been appalling. Horace Walpole described Bristol as 'the dirtiest great shop I ever saw'.

In 1753, scarcity of food and severe weather, plus widespread cattle disease, meant even higher bread and meat prices, and a new food riot broke out in Bristol. Again, on 21 May, rioters marched from Kingswood to the city centre, where the Council again attempted to disperse them with promises to reduce prices. But the crowd were incensed when they heard that grain was still being exported while domestic prices were kept high. Maddened by news that a ship, *The Lamb*, was preparing to sail to Dublin with 70 tons of wheat, they smashed the windows of the Council House and made their way to the quay to plunder the ship, but were charged by constables armed with staves, leaving several wounded and one rioter captured. The mob threatened further violence if the prisoner was not released, and rioting continued for several days as the horde grew to 900. They broke into Bridewell prison and released the prisoner, but one man was shot dead by a warder. As the fighting intensified, the cavalry arrived. A troop of Scots Greys sent from Gloucester charged the mob, killing and injuring over 50, with many more arrested. But the rioters themselves had taken 'five or six gentlemen' as hostages and carried them back to the coalpits. A couple of days later, the hostages were released, the authorities sent doctors to care for the wounded and a collection was organised by the townspeople for the miners and weavers. Few authorities favoured harsh punishment and the risk of 'rekindling the flames'. It was hoped that the disturbances would quieten down.

Two courts off Stillhouse Lane: St John's Buildings and The Arcade, which remained slum areas up to the end of the nineteenth century. Drawings by Samuel Loxton.
Courtesy of Bristol City Reference Library

For several more years, wheat for bread had to be supplemented by barley, peas, rice and potatoes. Even this was beyond the destitute, and some families of small tradesmen and craftsmen were reduced to eating bread made from potato flour. With people driven to desperation, food riots again rocked the city; the populace attacked butchers' shops in the High Street Market and carried off a quantity of meat; they also sacked a baker's shop, and when threatened with gunfire, the women shouted that they would have fresh butter and would 'live as well as ye gentry!' Meanwhile, Kingswood colliers seized several cartloads of corn on the way to market. Riots would continue to be a popular and effective way for people in Bristol to express disgust and despair at the authority's actions or inactions; the toll-bridge riots in 1793 left 11 protesters dead. But the worst violence that Bristol, and probably the entire country, experienced were the Reform Bill riots of 1831, when part of the city went up in flames, including Queen Square, and it is said that as many as 500 protestors were killed.

Living conditions among the poor in Bristol seemed to get worse rather than improve. Many worked in the coal mines, tanneries, glass and pottery factories, sugar refineries and cloth works – all of which were largely dangerous, monotonous and ill-paid professions. Life at home was not much better. Food ate up the bulk of the poor family's budget and fuel too was very expensive. Most labouring households still had an open fireplace with a large

A Recipe for Charity Soup

Soup kitchens were a regular sight in late eighteenth- and early nineteenth-century Bristol.

Half an ox cheek
sixpennyworth of fresh bones
ten large carrots
twelve turnips
three pounds of potatoes
eighteen leeks or onions
three quarts of split peas

Put the whole of these articles, together with any bones or meat trimmings or colde vegetables there may be in the larder, and any water that meat or poultry has been boiled in, into an iron pot with three gallons of cold water. Put it by the fire to boil up slowly, stir and skim often, let it simmer for six hours after it boils. Take out all the bones, stir in half an ounce of black pepper and a quarter pound of salt. The quantities will make ten quarts of soup and the cost will be about 5s.

cauldron in which to boil porridge or stews, mostly of root vegetables with perhaps a bit of fat bacon and pulses. Their diet continued to be meagre, with daily meals of bread and cheese and drinks of tea leaves – used over and over again, often with used, redried leaves added to fresh ones and also adulterated with other plant leaves such as willow and sloe. However, at least potatoes were now more commonly eaten. Those with access to a little land could grow some vegetables and many made seasonal trips into the countryside to forage for greens, nuts and berries.

The wage of a factory labourer was about 10-15 shillings a week, whilst 'common' labourers earned one-and-sixpence a day 'without victuals'. Children employed in cotton factories earned up to three shillings a week. One case is recorded of a 50-year-old Bristol labourer with a wife and two young children who worked in an inn as a horse keeper and porter. He earned nine shillings per week and his wife earned an occasional shilling by washing. The weekly family expenditure for bread, meat, butter, cheese, tea, potatoes, milk for the children, beer, candles, soap, onions and salt came to 8s 4½d, plus rent of 1s 2d and fuel at 1s 0d, which made a total of 10s 2d. So the family were short by more than one shilling before any amount was allowed for clothing and other essentials, which they possibly had to seek from various charities.

Fear of the workhouse or prison loomed large among the poor – no wonder, as the death rate in a Bristol workhouse was staggering. Bristol's city-centre Newgate prison was notorious with shackled children 'brought in for stealing a pound and a half of sugar' alongside brutal murderers. Many perished there from hunger and fever amid its filth and privations. Prisoners actually paid for their own food and drink, which was appalling (simply two pennyworth of black bread and gruel daily per head) and otherwise relied on the odd cartload of scraps such as salt fish, vegetables, potatoes and 'sixpenny loaves' and some donations of money.

Donating money, services and food has a long history in Bristol and the city's wealthy merchants had already long been known for their charitable works at this point. They left generous funds to pay for good deeds to commend their souls to heaven. As early as the Middle Ages, Bristol's wealthiest leading benefactors, such as John Whitson, John Carr and William Canynges, founded schools, a leper colony and almshouses. In 1613, Dr Thomas White founded the Temple Hospital almshouse, with room for eight men and two widows (whom he personally selected), and bestowed funds for an annual feast to be held at the hospital on 21 December, the Feast Day of Apostle Thomas. He left 40 shillings with precise instructions that the food should be 'plain', such as a baron of beef and apple pie flavoured with quince, and served on special pewter plates kept for the occasion. However, the dinner was eaten by the governors of the hospital and only the leftovers, 'which makes them an ample meal', were given to the 'poor and impotent people' to eat in the hospital kitchen. Four hundred years later, this dinner still takes place when Dr White's will is read out to guests, residents of the modern almshouses (who do now get to eat the dinner) and the lord mayor of Bristol. In 1737, the Bristol Infirmary was founded, with 78 Bristol citizens pledging between two and six guineas 'to benefit the poor sick' (possibly the first hospital for the sick built in a provincial city; the 'Royal' came in 1850). Patients were treated with a range of special diets. A 'wet diet' consisted of broth or milk pottage and a little pounded beef or mutton plus 'Rice Milk or Pap'. A 'dry diet' included bread and cheese and boiled rice with a pint of cider or beer. A 'fever diet' was little more than rice or barley gruel, sago, panado (bread boiled to a pulp in water and sweetened) and sage tea.

Edward Colston MP (1636-1721) was Bristol's best-known philanthropist. Although he made his fortune in London as a slave trader, he concentrated his charitable works in Bristol, the city of his birth. A lavish benefactor of schools, poorhouses, hospitals and retired seamen in the city, he declared that 'every helpless widow is my wife and her distressed orphans my children'. Colston purchased what had been John Young's Great House, which was by

The Colston Bun

Flour and butter in the proportions 8:1. The yeast is set to work with sugar and flour in a little warm milk for about 30 minutes. In the meantime, the butter is rubbed into the flour, together with a little sweet spice (cinnamon, allspice and nutmeg), plus grated lemon rind and a little dried fruit and candied peel; then the yeast mixture is stirred in, plus enough warm milk to produce a coherent dough. After rising, shaping, proving and marking, the buns are baked at 220°C for 20-25 minutes. They are glazed with sugar syrup whilst still warm. (Recipe courtesy of Laura Mason)

then being used as a sugar refinery, and turned it into a school that trained 100 'Poor Boys' for a life at sea. But life at Colston School was pretty spartan: for breakfast, bread and butter, bread and broth or bread and gruel; for dinner, bread and beef or hot bread and butter or pease pudding or bread and boiled mutton; supper was either bread and cheese or milk pottage. Boys were supplied with brewing utensils plus barrels and a small bowl called a *porringer*. But this was considerably better than Kingswood school, founded by John Wesley for sons of dissenters. Here the boys rose at four in the morning and had to survive on a breakfast of milk or water porridge until the midday dinner of meat with apple pudding, except on Fridays when they had vegetables and dumplings; supper was meagre helpings of bread and cheese with milk. Few girls received any schooling at all, though some from wealthy families were sent to boarding schools, where they learned to read and write a little and occasionally to spell, but were expected to devote most of their learning to dancing, singing, music and needlework. Bristol's Red Maids' School was once in Red Lodge, adjacent to the Great House. It was founded in 1634 from the bequest of John Whitson, mayor and MP of Bristol, to house the orphaned or destitute daughters of the city's freemen or burgesses. Girls were taught to read but not to write, and their needlework was sold to pay for their keep.

Charitable handouts in the form of buns seem to have been a longstanding tradition in Bristol. The round-shaped Colston Bun, said to have been popularised by the benefactor Edward Colston, was made with a yeast dough flavoured with dried fruit, candied peel and sweet spices. The bun came in two sizes: 'dinner plate', with eight wedge marks on the surface, and a small 'ha'penny starver'. After the annual Charter Day Service at Bristol Cathedral, each schoolboy at the service was given one large bun to take home to his

St Michael's Church, April 1958. Tuppenny starvers are still handed out to children on Easter Tuesday

family plus the 'starver' to stave off his immediate hunger. This bun is still traditionally baked on Charter Day and distributed to Bristol schoolchildren by the Colston Society. Similarly, in 1748, Peter and Mary Davies left money in their wills for traditional large, fruited buns called 'tuppenny starvers' to be handed out to choristers in the medieval church of St Michael the Archangel on the Mount Without. No one knows the origins of this particular tradition, but schoolchildren at St Michael's School still enjoy the buns on Easter Tuesday. For poor children and their families, a hard, sweet bun taken home and dipped in bowls of sweetened tea was perhaps the beginning of the great British passion for sugar.

SWEETEN TO TASTE – SUGAR AND SLAVERY

Once a luxury, by the eighteenth century sugar had become an essential part of almost everyone's diet. It created a revolution in eating habits and was consumed on a daily basis in ever-greater quantities in a wider variety of ways. Sugar was now used to sweeten coffee, tea and cocoa, to make cakes, jams and preserves and to produce puddings and confectionery. It turned breakfast into a sweet rather than savoury meal, with hot sweetened beverages, treacle drizzled on porridge and sugared breads spread with marmalade. Dinner now ended with a seductive sweet course. Cheap rum, a by-product of sugar, began to be a popular alternative to the 'devilish gin' and was even thought to be healthy; the rich served it as punch, the poor drank it neat and the navy distributed daily rum rations to its men. Now the poor not only demanded white bread but something sweet to spread on it and to sweeten their drinks. 'Sugar is so generally in use by the assistance of tea', explained a 1774 report, 'that even the poor wretches living in almshouses will not be without it.' Towards the end of the eighteenth century it was estimated that a typical poor family in town would spend as much as 6 per cent of its income on sweetening their food and drinks. Sugar, tea and tobacco became synonymous with British working-class life.

But there was nothing sweet about the sugar trade. Britain led the world in importing more sugar than any other country; the 'white gold' had become the driving force of its wealth and the most important product of its rapidly expanding and now almost-global commerce. As the country's second port, Bristol's trade with British-owned sugar plantations in the West Indies kept no fewer than 20 refineries busy in the city. There were huge fortunes to be made from it, though what really produced such fabulous wealth was not sugar itself but the trade in slaves needed to grow it.

For centuries, slavery had been practised almost everywhere, from China and India to Europe and Africa. But the new transatlantic slave trade was on a different scale and made fortunes for many people, most of whom never saw a single slave. Trading in slaves was nothing new to Bristolians, who had been shipping slaves and indentured servants through its port since the Middle Ages. Shiploads of political prisoners and unfortunates of all kinds passed from the port of Bristol to a life of slavery in the colonies. The Victorian historian, Thomas Macaulay, commented in *History of England* (1848) that 'Nowhere was this system found in such active and extensive operation as at Bristol. Even the first magistrates of that city were not ashamed to enrich themselves by so odious a commerce.'

The first sugar plantations were manned with European slaves, or bondspeople (Portuguese sugar plantations in Madeira used convicts, debtors and Jews who refused to convert to Christianity), but they proved unable to stand the rigours of plantation life and many sickened and died long before the period of bondage to which they were condemned was over. It soon became evident that if the plantation system was to succeed, some other source of labour supply must be found. As early as 1619, a cargo of enslaved Africans was landed in Virginia, and by the middle of the century slaves shipped from Africa were to be found in almost all of the southern mainland and island colonies. It was believed that their capacity for enduring tropical heat, to which

Planting sugar cane in Antigua, a back-breaking job. Gangs included both men and women. *The History of Sugar*, Noel Deerr, 1949

they were accustomed, their docility and great physical strength suited them for the work. But overcrowded ships and appalling conditions meant that nearly half of each human 'cargo' did not survive the voyage. The rest were doomed to a short, harsh existence working on a plantation cutting sugar cane or in the sugar-boiling and -processing plants.

Anyone who could get into the slave trade was virtually guaranteed to make their fortune. But at first it wasn't straightforward. Through its Royal African Company, London held a monopoly on all British trade with Africa, and only ships owned by this company could trade for gold, ivory, spices, dyes and slaves. Although Bristol shipowners were involved in trading slaves as early as the 1670s, they were doing it illegally and risked losing their ship and cargo if caught. But Bristol merchants were long used to illegal and underhand activities and thought nothing of taking risks and flouting the law if the profits were big enough. Bristol's Society of Merchant Venturers was desperate to have their share of the new market and legalise their position and kept up pressure on Parliament to change the rules. Finally, in 1698, the monopoly was ended and for the first time a Bristol-owned ship sailed freely to the African coast – it was aptly named *The Beginning*.

For Bristol citizens it was indeed the beginning of an incredible bonanza to be gained from what was known as the transatlantic 'Triangular Trade' because of the three trading points of the voyage. This involved loading a ship in Bristol with a range of desirable goods which were taken to the coast of Africa and used to barter for slaves. When a sufficient number of slaves had been collected, they were loaded into the empty cargo holds and shipped across the Atlantic to the Caribbean islands, where they were sold for work in British sugar and tobacco plantations. The triangle was completed when the ship was loaded with sugar, tobacco, rum and other exotic goods bought in Africa, such as ivory, gold and palm oil, and brought back to Bristol for the investors to sell. If all went well there were profits to be made on each leg of the triangle. It

A sugar factory in Antigua showing the different stages of boiling sugar, a highly skilled and dangerous job as boiling sugar could burn a victim to death. *The History of Sugar*, Noel Deerr, 1949

was a city tradition that the owner of the first ship of the season to bring sugar back from the Caribbean celebrated by buying wine for all his friends. (Instead of doing the triangle, a few ships sailed north to Newfoundland, where they bought an inferior kind of salt cod known as the 'West India Cure' – to take to the southern plantations to feed the slaves – and returned to Newfoundland with rum and sugar for the fishery workers and northern colonies.)

Bristol shipowners always kept careful accounts. For example, the slave ship *Africa* kept records of the names of companies which invested in a voyage or supplied the ship with everything required for the voyage, plus a list of goods taken on the outward passage to be sold to African traders in exchange for enslaved people. Thomas Baker, the captain of the *Africa*, was instructed to trade along the west coast of Africa 'buying all the healthy young negroes that offer, as well ivory, gold and megella [pepper]'. All kinds of local industries flourished because their goods were bartered for slaves or they provided services and products necessary for supplying and maintaining slaving ships and their crews. So, local factories produced copper sheathing to protect the hulls of slave ships from tropical conditions. Great local brass and iron foundries made tools, guns and ornaments; the city's famed glassworks produced beads and bottles (bottles of beer and cider went out to the Caribbean and were returned filled with rum); the potteries turned out porcelain tableware – all fuelled with Bristol coal. Workers made clothes out of woollen cloth from Somerset and Gloucestershire and food industries prospered: bakers made *hardtack* (bread) to feed the crew and slaves and grocers supplied hard cheese and barrels of salt meat and fish. Soapmakers, tanneries, rope- and sailmakers, ships' chandlers and so on all increased their business thanks to the slave trade. Thus almost every middle-class citizen in Bristol benefitted financially from slavery, and not just the wealthy investors, shipowners, merchants and plantation owners. Others who profited and were kept employed included the Bristol banks who invested in the trade; insurance companies covering voyages against

Huge barrels of raw sugar are unloaded at the Bristol Quay and sent on to the sugar houses for refining.
Courtesy Bristol City Reference Library

loss; lawyers who drew up trade contracts; customs officers, tax inspectors and their clerks; and armies of seamen, dock workers and general labourers.

And when a ship arrived home, the raw sugar was taken to refineries and barrels of rum and *tierces* (wooden drums) of tobacco were dragged away on sledges to the warehouses. (Some tobacco, sugar and rum brought from previous voyages to the Caribbean was also used as bribes and gifts for slave dealers in Africa.) Other goods that came back – such as cotton, rice, indigo dye, pimento (pepper), ginger, cocoa, coffee, timber, ivory and palm oil – were sent all around the country to be sold.

For ten years, while Bristol was the leading British port, it has been estimated that up to half a million enslaved Africans were traded by Bristol merchants: roughly one-fifth of all slaves transported in British ships. During its heyday, Bristol was sending out 20 ships a year on the year-long round trip, ranging in size from only 27 tons to a mighty 420 tons with wide hulls able to hold up to 600 enslaved Africans. Almost every famous Bristol name was associated with the slave trade. Several generations of Bristol families owned large estates on British Caribbean islands such as Barbados, Jamaica, St Kitts and Nevis and many had a member of the family living there and managing them.

So it was that, around Christmas 1765, John Pretor-Pinney sailed out to

Nevis, where he embarked on a long career as a planter, merchant and 'man of affairs'. He had inherited the plantation from a distant cousin, who had left the estate in a sorry state. It was a particularly tumultuous period when England was at war with France, and plantation owners were often absent from their estates, but Pinney planned to rebuild his family's fortunes. He vowed not to succumb to the usual seductions of a planter's life: drinking rum, cockfighting and whoring with slave women. As he wrote:

> I am determined not to follow the Vices of ye Country, but to live the Life of an Honest, Sober, and Diligent Planter, for yt was my only Motive of coming here, and it is the only step I can take to ease myself of my present encumbrances.

Pinney threw himself into his work until he had paid off the debts and the plantations were once again thriving. He married the daughter of another Nevis planter and built a new house and several new sugar mills. He cleared uncultivated land, planted more sugar cane, purchased mules, slaves and provisions and, within a few years, was shipping huge quantities of sugar to Bristol.

Planter families like the Pinneys were not usually directly involved in shipping and selling slaves, but they bought slaves and used them on their sugar plantations, where life was brutal: branding, flogging, whipping for runaways and even the use of necklocks on children was commonplace on Nevis. In the same vein, food provision was meagre. A low-grade salt cod known as 'green cod' was shipped from Newfoundland to feed the slaves, who otherwise subsisted on mealie corn, potatoes or cassava root, rice and yams. They supplemented their rations with a few chickens or a goat and grew vegetables on the small patch of land beside the thatched huts in which they lived.

Pinney's views on slavery were initially undecided and he expressed concerns about the 'rights and wrongs' of owning slaves but later convinced himself that it was acceptable. In a letter dated 1765 he wrote: 'Since my Arrival, I've purchased 9 Negro Slaves in St Kitts and can assure you I was shock'd at the first appearance of human flesh expos'd for Sale.' But he was quickly converted to the necessity of having them, saying 'it is as impossible for a Man to make Sugar without the assistance of Negroes, as to make Bricks without Straw'.

Plantations in the West Indies were dependent on almost everything they needed being sent out to them. Ships arrived in spring with, for those running the plantation, new furniture, curtains and bed linen, fine china and glass for the dining room and all kinds of household effects and kitchen equipment, plus clothing and personal necessities for the growing family. There were orders for new equipment and tools, building materials such as lime, timber and bricks, fishing lines, equipment for boiling sugar, hogsheads, soap, candles and 'bushel bags'. Pinney enjoyed his food and missed the good things from home. He ordered English bacon, cheeses, butter, spices and French and Spanish wines. He wrote to his wine dealer in Cadiz requesting a butt of the very best sherry: 'as it is for our own use, we hope it will be superior to the sale wines usually to be met with'. Some fruits and more exotic things came from English estates in Virginia and Pennsylvania. However, letters of complaint were regularly sent back to suppliers, including one to 'The Shippers of the Pickles which were entirely spoil'd by being ill-pack'd & having no Stoppers nor Covers save a little Brown paper.' An order of '2 Glocester and 1 Cheddar cheeses' was not up to scratch; 'the cheese was not so good as I could have wished, pray send always the best that can be procured, it being for my own table and what I am fond of'. Mrs Pinney, meanwhile, kept a vegetable garden and grew as many varieties of green stuff that could cope with the climate. In a letter home she wrote: 'We are pestered in our houses with many disagreeable insects, such as flyes, cockroch's, scorpions, centipedes etc the two last are venomous.' But there were many things to enjoy on the island and Tom Wedgwood (son of the abolitionist), who later stayed on Nevis, described it as a paradise of 'birds singing on all sides of me – oranges by thousands close to the house – a supper on land-crabs …'.

The outbreak of the American War in 1775, when the French allied themselves with America, caused considerable disruption. As American and French privateers roamed the sea around the West Indies, war disrupted the supply lines and food became very expensive and difficult to obtain. By March 1778, several hundred slaves had died from hunger on Nevis, but it seems that Pinney managed to stave off a worse famine by planting additional food crops instead of sugar cane. Despite several attacks by the French, Pinney carried on and was able to keep the plantations operating profitably. By 1783, however, he had had enough and announced that he was going home to supervise the education of his five children in England.

On 27 June 1787, another character stepped into the slavery story as Thomas Clarkson, a young Cambridge graduate, came riding his horse westward into Bristol. Over six feet tall, with thick red hair and direct, intense blue eyes, Clarkson was an imposing figure, yet he expressed fears for his own safety in Bristol. He was on a fact-finding tour of the major slaving cities, to find eyewitnesses who would testify before Parliament and whip up support among Dissenters and radicals in the provinces. Visiting Bristol, whose warehouses were bursting with slave-grown products just arrived from the West Indies and Americas, was going to be a dangerous business. As Clarkson approached through a summer heat haze, he recalled how the city seemed to shimmer and grow enormous:

> I began now to tremble, for the first time, at the arduous task I had undertaken, of attempting to subvert one of the branches of the commerce of the great place which was then before me ... I questioned whether I should even get out of it alive.

Clarkson was, however, surprised to find that few Bristolians were proud of the trade: 'every body seemed to execrate it, though no one thought of its abolition'. He soon found help and support among Quakers, Anglicans, Unitarians, and even the Society of Merchant Venturers allowed him access to muster rolls of seamen on slave ships. His most useful ally and guide turned out to be the landlord of a local tavern, the Seven Stars, who boarded seamen but refused any association with the slavers. The landlord escorted Clarkson round the public houses in Marsh Street where crews were recruited and where Clarkson himself witnessed how landlords and ships' mates plied and stupe-fied sailors with drink, or encouraged them to spend beyond their means until signing on for a slave voyage remained the only alternative to imprisonment for debt. The most harrowing testimonies came from sailors who had suffered appalling violence and sickness on these voyages. Evidence of the cruelty and conditions suffered by the slaves themselves had to be found among the seamen and Clarkson recorded hundreds of incidences of brutality, murder and callous treatment against slaves. But finding any man willing to testify in public was proving almost impossible. Only a few brave ships' surgeons were prepared to describe the barbarity of the trade openly. Slave captains were even less prepared to speak and shunned Clarkson as if he 'had been a mad dog'. In many places he found open hostility – 'I shall never forget the savage looks which these people gave me', he wrote – and it became increasingly difficult to find anyone willing to help him. Fortunately, his hard work and zeal had so impressed those in Bristol sympathetic to his cause that he was able to leave his campaign in local hands.

But the slave business in Bristol was already in decline, and the city's share of the Africa trade had dwindled, mostly as a result of the economic crises of 1793, which hit Bristol particularly hard with numerous bankruptcies, including that of several slave-ship owners. Liverpool survived such economic woes and recovered quickly, but Bristol seems to have accepted the inevitable. Between 1794 and 1804, only 24 slaving ships left Bristol, a fraction of the Liverpool and London sailings, and Bristol refineries were reduced to getting supplies of sugar from Liverpool. When, in 1806, Parliament finally resolved to abolish the trade, Bristol newspapers reported favourably on the event; Felix Farley, the Quaker newspaper owner, hailed the abolition of a trade 'so long the disgrace of a civilized nation'.

ROAST BEEF AND BOILED PUDDING

On his return to Bristol, John Pinney built himself a house on Great George Street, off Park Street, overlooking the cathedral and city docks. The house was built of stone, with large windows and high-ceilinged rooms furnished to combine elegance with utility. The servants slept in the attics and worked below ground in the well-equipped kitchen and storerooms. The family had brought back two Africans from Nevis to work as servants: Pero Jones (a slave) was John Pinney's personal servant, while Fanny Coker (a free woman), who had been brought up by Mrs Pinney 'with great Tenderness', was her lady's maid and companion. This was unusual as slaves were never brought into Bristol – apart from a small number of black servants who 'were dressed up in fancy livery' and kept as exotic ornaments, objects of curiosity and 'luxury items' in the households of well-to-do families.

Mrs Pinney, who had spent most of her life in the Caribbean, had a lot to get used to apart from the local attitude to black people, not least the English cooking. Now that middle-class townswomen had opened their eyes to the new ideas in cooking and exotic ingredients arriving at the docks and in the markets, one might have expected there to be a revolution at the Georgian dinner table. Quality and quantity of food had improved and kitchens had evolved into sophisticated and well-equipped engine rooms capable of producing complex and elaborate dishes. So why was there so much talk of roast beef and boiled pudding? Where were the colourful show-off dishes of Norman and Elizabethan town life and why were the burghers of provincial Bristol so satisfied with their 'plain fare'? It was partly the fault of the French and their intermittent wars with England during this time, culminating in the great alarm caused by the French Revolution in 1789. French chefs and sophisticated French food had once been *à la mode*, but now 'Frenchified stuff' was frowned on and eating English was considered more patriotic. Whether or not this was entirely the case, certainly a robust, richly filling, generously spread table was becoming popular. The middle and upper classes usually ate at least three times a day: at 7 am, around noon and at 6 pm, with possibly a social gathering for tea mid afternoon. When the Pinney family gathered for a family meal, they ate in an intimate and comfortable dining room, sitting on Chippendale chairs and eating off an elegant dining table made from West Indies mahogany, with fine porcelain from China, bone china from Josiah Wedg-

Roast beef and boiled pudding. Peter Brears

wood's potteries, silverware, cut-glass decanters and wine glasses from Italy filled with French and Spanish wines. A typical dinner menu was: pea soup, sole with oyster sauce or potted salmon, a nice piece of roast beef with a plum pudding, a fine neck of roast pork and apple sauce, some hashed turkey and wild duck or fried rabbit with some vegetable side dishes. This was followed by a dessert course of sweet pies, lemon cream and trifle (trifle became a particular favourite in Bristol, where sherry-flavoured cream was used). After dessert with a glass of sweet wine, the ladies withdrew, leaving the men to their cigars and port wine, which had become a fashionable after-dinner drink. Later they joined the ladies in the 'withdrawing room' for conversation and card games. It all sounds rather civilised, if a little dull.

The British were particularly proud of the 'Roast beef of Old England', and by the 1740s, roast beef and plum pudding had become national dishes. Meat was standard fare for those who could afford it and was cooked in many ways, such as hashes, fricassees, *collops* (slices) and collared cuts as well as stews and, of course, the roasts. Foreign visitors to Britain, such as Monsieur Henri Misson from France, were amazed at the amount of meat consumed:

Among the middling sort of people they had ten or twelve sorts of common meats which infallibly takes their turns at their tables, and two dishes are their dinners: a pudding … and a piece of roast beef.

Steamed or boiled puddings were a very English phenomenon, taking the place of cereal pottage as a starchy filler (potatoes were still not eaten every day). The pudding cloth was a great invention going back to Elizabethan times, and making it possible to mix flour, milk, eggs, butter, sugar, suet, bone marrow and dried fruits into a whole range of hot, filling and nutritious dishes at little cost or effort. All you had to do was fill the cloth with the mixture, tie it tight at both ends and plunge it into a boiling pot which might already be simmering with meat and vegetables, where it could cook gently for hours. The pudding varied in texture and quality from light, moist and custardy to heavily fruited oatmeal. Some puddings began to be made without meat, using just dried fruit and spices. These boiled puddings became a mainstay of English cooking and were often remarked on by foreign visitors to England. Per Kalm, the Swedish naturalist who took a great interest in English food and cooking, observed on his visit in 1748: 'the art of cooking as practised by most Englishmen does not extend much beyond roast beef and plum pudding'. Of the puddings, Henri Misson also noted that: 'They bake them in the oven, they boil them with the meat, they make them fifty several ways: Blessed Be He That Invented Pudding, for it is a manna that hits the palates of all sorts of people – [and the English] are never weary of it.'

Lashings of cream were used in everyday dishes and everything was literally 'swimming in butter'. Sugar remained king, but many of the old spices went out of fashion except nutmeg, which was then the favourite. Pickles, ketchups and sweet-sour flavours became popular. Vegetables were finally beginning to come into their own as an accompaniment or side dish: peas with duck or pork, carrots and boiled beef, cabbage and calf's head, cucumber sauce with lamb, and turnips with mutton. Even the potato entered the middle-class dining room: boiled with a jug of melted butter to pour over them, roasted in the dripping pan, sliced and cooked with herring, fried in butter, mashed with cream, sugar and dried fruits, and used in boiled puddings. Vegetables were still overcooked but not as much as in the days of the pottage, when they were simmered for several hours until all the goodness was gone.

The eighteenth-century diet of meat, fats, salt, sugar and alcohol (and smoking) took a very heavy toll on health. Gout, diabetes and heart and liver disease were all common complaints. Drinking in the eighteenth century was particularly widespread. Strong drink was cheap and easily available (although French wines and brandy were heavily taxed and expensive). 'Heroic drinking' was a term given to eighteenth-century excess, when heavy drinking and eating was regarded as admirable and manly. When a Mr Reeves opened his new hotel in Bristol, he invited the mayor and 22 aldermen and common councillors to celebrate. The bacchanalian powers of the party may be judged from the wine bill: '12 bottles of sherry, 12 of port, 12 of hock, 20 of claret and 6 of champagne'; a grand total of 62 bottles for 23 diners. The necessity to entertain visiting royals continued to be expensive. In 1738, on his visit to

Bristol, the Prince of Wales was given 'a sumptuous banquet' at the Merchants' Hall, with a similar feast a year later for the Duke of Gloucester. 'Shampeighn' was probably drunk for the first time in Bristol when served to the prince and princess in 1738, at a cost of 6 guineas. Coffee houses gradually fell out of favour and men started to meet in their own clubhouses, where they consumed huge quantities of claret, sherry and 'Canary', 'Alicante' and 'Rhenish' wines and kept plentiful stocks of distilled brandy and rum, as well as perry and cider, ale and porter. The Duke of Norfolk, an 'eccentric gastronome', was reported to have dined with a party of gentlemen members of Bristol's Common Council and other leading citizens at the Rose and Crown, which was famous for its Saturday tripe and beefsteak dinners. The duke is said to have 'eaten like Ajax, and drunk with twenty-aldermanic power'. The *Bristol Times* reported that, when His Grace tried to leave through a narrow alley, due to his enormous size he knocked over an oyster stall owned by an old woman 'who poured choleric abuse on the convivial nobleman'. The example set by the richer classes was followed, as far as means would allow, by the poorer, who kept the many hundreds of public houses in profitable trade.

'CULTURAL DOLDRUMS' AND 'NARROW NOTIONS'

Visitors had often remarked on Bristol's materialism and dogged pursuit of profit, noting that its inhabitants held no ideas beyond the business of making money. The poet and satirist Alexander Pope, who came to 'take the waters' in 1739, thought the city 'very unpleasant', with 'no Civilized Company in it. Only the Collector of the Customs would have brought me acquainted with the Merchants, of whom I hear no great Character'. John Wesley, whose preaching had such a dramatic and lasting effect on religious life in Bristol, was similarly unimpressed. He wrote to a friend: 'I often wonder at the people of Bristol. They are so honest, yet so dull; 'tis scarce possible to strike any fire into them.' Thomas Cox, in his *Magna Britannia*, was similarly depressed by the narrow-minded commercialising:

> Bristol is very populous, but the people give themselves up to trade so entirely that nothing of the politeness and gaiety of Bath is to be seen here; all are in a hurry, running up and down with cloudy looks and busy faces, loading, carrying and unloading goods and merchandizes of all sorts from place to place; the trade of many nations is drawn hither by the industry and opulency of the people.

In *Bristol: A Satire*, local poet Robert Lovell stressed the blinkered business interests of the city and the need to know how stocks and shares are doing.

Done to a Turn

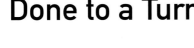

Georgian houses were built with great attention to innovation as well as grand design. The kitchen in particular came in for a lot of modern ideas. New developments in iron-work and mechanisation were quickly adopted in these up-to-the-minute kitchens.

At the beginning of the eighteenth century, most kitchens were fairly simple, with some utensils and equipment made by the local blacksmith. During the building boom 50 years later, residents could choose from a huge variety of mass-produced ovens, ranges, tools, pots, dishes and glasses. The kitchen range in these grand Georgian houses had come a long way from the open, roaring fires of the Middle Ages: it was now sophisticated and ingenious. The old open wood fire had given way to a coal fire basket, which gradually developed into the 'grate' or 'range'. Now the heat from the fire could be controlled by winding adjustable sides or 'cheeks' inwards using a rack-and-pinion mechanism. Trivets fastened to the cheek tops could swing out and over the fire to support small pans. In front of the fire could be a metal screen with highly polished surfaces to reflect heat and cook meats, puddings, bread and cakes better. Some smart kitchens had a separate stove, giving a gentler heat on which to stew slowly or make sauces; this made it easier and pleasanter for the cook, who no longer had to bend over the hot

flames whilst stirring her sauces or gravy. One step better was the Dutch oven, or 'hastener', a large metal box with a polished interior – the beginnings of the modern oven. This reflected the heat so efficiently that the cook could roast a joint of meat and bake a batter pudding (later called Yorkshire pudding) at the same time. Meanwhile, the ubiquitous cauldron still hung over the fire, where meat, puddings and nets of vegetables could all simmer away in the same water, which was later used for soups or gruel.

Advances in the iron industry meant new and improved equipment was being introduced and housewives and their builders had to be alert to the numerous advertisements if they were to keep up. The first cast-iron kitchen range was invented in 1780 by Thomas Robinson. It had a central grate, a closed oven with a hinged door on one side and a tank for heating water on the other. By the end of the century, the inventor Count Rumford had devised a more elaborate design that included an early version of the modern hob.

Open-fire roasting was still the favourite way to cook meat. It continued to be done by rotating the joint before the fire, either suspended from a hook or fastened on an iron spit that not only turned the meat before the fire but conducted heat to the centre of the joint, ensuring it was thoroughly cooked throughout. The melting fat collected in a wide, shallow pan and was ladled over the meat to 'baste' it. Now, instead of overheated turnspit boys hand-turning and basting, the spits rested on a pair of 'andirons' at the front of the basket and were mostly turned

mechanically. Poorer households used a 'danglespit' or 'poor man's jack'. With this, the meat was held on a hook tied to a length of string that was twisted hard and suspended from the mantelpiece. As the twists unravelled, the piece of meat spun slowly before the fire. Roasting jacks of varying degrees of sophistication were used; they incorporated various spring-wound or weight-driven devices, often regulated by clockwork, to keep the spits turning continuously until the joint was 'done to a turn'.

Curiously, an old method of turning spits seems to have been retained in Bristol long after it had disappeared from other parts of the country. The 'turnspit dog' was described by the naturalist Thomas Bewick as 'a long-bodied animal with short, crooked legs, with a tail curled upon its back and frequently spotted black on grey'. These dogs were

placed inside a dogwheel connected to a grooved wheel on the spit; they had to keep running so that the meat spit kept turning. One visitor to Bristol in the seventeenth century wrote that there is 'scarce a house that hath not a dogge to turn the spitte in a little wooden wheele'. The dogs were still running in 1774, when the poet Robert Southey deplored the cruel way they were trained. He claimed that they were put in the wheel with a burning coal which they could only avoid by running at 'full gallop'. Happily, by 1807, Southey declared the turnspit dog was almost extinct.

How goes sugar? What's the price of rum?
What ships arrived? And how are stocks today?
Who's dead? Who's broken? And who's run away?

What Bristol needed were some fresh voices and ideas from the world outside and a more colourful society to spice things up a bit. Perhaps the best attraction for drawing in interesting people was the Hotwell Spa, which became part of the annual season and for a while was one of England's best-frequented and most crowded watering places, where scores of notable members of society could be found every season (Hotwell/s referred to the warm springs bubbling up in that part of Bristol, whose waters were said to benefit the health). Bristol newspapers began reporting the arrival of aristocracy and gentry, including Sarah, Duchess of Marlborough, the Duke of York and Lady Spencer, who were followed by many of the fashionable elite; even some of the literary and artistic jet set of the Georgian era were tempted to take the Bristol waters, such as Jonathan Swift, Daniel Defoe, Franz Joseph Haydn – and Alexander Pope, as mentioned.

The Bristol Hotwell was a summer resort and Bath a winter one, so that many traders moved their shops from Bath to Bristol to catch the summer trade. The spa was also cheap – lodgings cost just 10 shillings (about £42.50 in today's money) a week, servants half price. There were two assembly rooms, one of which boasted a 'man cook' who served nourishing breakfasts and elegant teas. There were numerous genteel outings, many of which involved food and drink. For example, on fine days visitors could ride up to the hamlet of Clifton and drink milk fresh from the cow before perhaps continuing to the Downs to watch horse racing and cricket. Another popular outing was to cross the river at Rownham Ferry and walk to the 'sweet and wholesome village of Ashton to eat strawberries and raspberries with cream; a delicious repast'.

As well as those who came for pleasure there were, of course, invalids; soon there were dozens of rival physicians who claimed that the water could cure everything from 'feeble brains and pimply faces' to 'old sores', as well as diabetes and tuberculosis, the great scourge of the time. Clean drinking water was still at a premium and, although Hotwell water tasted rather chalky, it was reputed to retain its potency longer than others. The traveller Celia Fiennes once described it as 'warm as new milk and much of that sweetness'. Thousands of bottles were exported around the world, helping to support the local glass-making industry – Defoe noted that there were more glass houses in Bristol than in London. (A new artificial mineral water was developed around this time by Swiss businessman Jacob Schweppe, sold in egg-shaped stone bottles. Later, in 1812, he set up a Bristol branch of his business in Dowry Square.)

Gargantuan Dinners at the Bush Inn

The Bush Inn, in Corn Street (on the site of today's imposing Lloyds TSB building), was one of Bristol's celebrated coaching inns. Under its most famous landlord John Weeks it was renowned for its turtles and for its Gargantuan dinners.

The bill of fare at Christmas would occupy half a column in the local press, and on at least one occasion contained 155 items.

In 1788 a London newspaper reported that 'any person who calls for three-penny worth of liquor has the run of the larder, and may eat as much as he pleases for nothing. Last Christmas Day they sold 3,000 single glasses of punch before dinner'. For casual Christmas visitors there was a mighty baron of cold beef, weighing about 350lbs, flanked by correspondingly liberal supplies of mutton, ham and other meats.

The inn's coaching enterprises attracted no less attention. In April 1775, John Weeks advertised a flyer post chaise service to London in sixteen hours – a feat which apparently 'plunged old-fashioned travellers in equal astonishment and terror'. The fare was 3d a mile, and the high speed coaches carried only four passengers each.

Edmund Burke's supporters used the inn during their victorious election campaign of 1774, and in *Pickwick Papers* Charles Dickens had Mr Winkle stay here when visiting Bristol in search of Arabella Allen.

The grand houses in Bristol's smarter areas began to put on 'London airs' with the latest fashions in entertainments, clothing, furnishing – and food. Polite society went in their carriages to visit the pleasure gardens, assembly rooms, concert halls and theatres (the King Street Theatre Royal boasted top actors such as David Garrick and Mrs Siddons). Some wealthier houseowners had beautiful gardens designed for them. Daniel Defoe, one of Bristol's fiercest critics, conceded in *A Tour through England & Wales* that there were by then 'many genteel houses of entertainment all about the city, with neat walks and gardens, and very good accommodations'.

But Bristol needed more than society airs to lift itself out of what had long been a cultural doldrums. Happily, by the 1790s, the city was emerging from the backwater of provincial merchants, lawyers and shopkeepers with their 'Damn'd narrow notions' – as Bristol poet Thomas Chatterton had despairingly described them 25 years earlier. Bristol now had a thriving community of liberal-minded 'Unitarians' that drew in writers, scientists, publishers, educators and campaigners and injected a degree of free-thinking culture. The Unitarians, who represented the backbone of the Dissenting tradition in England, were strongly influenced by the ideas of the European Enlightenment, with its emphasis on the physical sciences and political reform. Every city had its Dissenting society; Unitarians owned many leading newspapers, journals and publishing houses, were associated with radical causes such as freedom of the press and the abolition of the slave trade and regarded themselves as the progressive intellectual elite. Bristol now also acquired newspapers and places of a Unitarian or intellectual flavour, such as the popular, long-running *Felix Farley's Bristol Journal*, a number of bookshops and The Bristol Library Society, recently opened for use by 'intellectual gentlemen' – and a few ladies. The Philosophical and Literary Institute in Park Street was a sort of university where lectures could be heard by a rising new outward-looking, intellectual elite living in the fashionable suburbs of Hotwells and Clifton. In 1795, Bristol even found itself briefly at the centre of the English Romantic Movement, affording some interesting culinary links and insights along the way.

Joseph Cottle, a small, shy man with a bad limp, and a Unitarian, minor poet and publisher, kept a bookshop in Wine Street that became the meeting place and centre of Bristol's progressive circle. Cottle's shop was also about to become, for a brief couple of years, the most important bookshop in England.

William Wordsworth, then a struggling young poet, was friends with the sons of sugar merchant John Pinney, Frederick and Azariah. The Pinneys offered William and his sister Dorothy the use of the family's country house in Dorset, where he could work in peace. Before moving to Dorset, Wordsworth stayed for five weeks at the Pinneys' house at Great George Street in Bristol, and it was during this time that Wordsworth met Joseph Cottle, who immediately offered to publish his work. It was in Cottle's bookshop too that William Wordsworth was introduced to Samuel Taylor Coleridge, which marked the start of a lifelong and hugely productive relationship between the two greatest poets of their generation. Also, Bristol-born poet Robert Southey had recently been studying in Oxford, along with another Bristol poet, Robert Lovell. There they met Samuel Taylor Coleridge and began a passionate, youthful dream of setting up a commune in America where they could practise a spiritual and political way of life which they called Pantisocracy. In June 1794, Coleridge paid a visit to Bristol, where Southey introduced him to his literary and revolutionary friends in the city including Cottle, who was already publishing poems by Lovell, Wordsworth and Southey. Cottle immediately offered to publish anything by Coleridge, who impetuously decided to stay in Bristol.

The young poets made their first commune in a small apartment in College

The Measure and Transport of Wine, attributed to Antoine Verard c.1528, Paris. Barrels of wine are being checked before shipment from France. Bibliotheque Historique de la Ville de Paris / Archives Charmet / The Bridgeman Art Library

Still Life With Confections, Clara Peeters c.1615.
A large scalloped-edge marchpane decorated with coloured comfits is surrounded by plates of knotted 'jumballs' and flowers made of sugar paste.
Courtesy www.bluffton.edu/womenartists

Turtle, various peppers including Jamaica pepper and the pineapple were among the exotic new food introductions featured in *Elegancies of Jamaica*, by Rev. John Lindsay (1758-1771). Courtesy: Bristol Museum Natural Sciences Collection

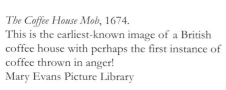

The Coffee House Mob, 1674.
This is the earliest-known image of a British
coffee house with perhaps the first instance of
coffee thrown in anger!
Mary Evans Picture Library

This painting of Broad Quay,
Bristol, attributed to Philip
Vandyke c.1780, shows the busy
quay with dockers unloading a
ship using the dockside crane
and merchants discussing
business amongst the workmen
and shoppers. Only sledges
were allowed to carry
merchandise in order to protect
the cellars underground.
Courtesy Bristol Museums,
Galleries & Archives

The oyster women's shed on Welsh Back was always busy. Along with beef, pudding and turtle, oysters were eaten in huge quantities. George Delamotte, *Oyster Women's Shed, Welsh Back*, (1824). Courtesy Bristol Museums, Galleries & Archives

The Cloak-Room, Clifton Assembly Rooms, 1817. An oil painting by Rolinda Sharples features many of her friends and patrons and includes her mother and herself preparing for an evening of socialising. Courtesy Bristol Museums, Galleries & Archives

A turnspit dog at work in a kitchen in Newcastle Emlyn, South Wales. A watercolour by Thomas Rowlandson, 1790. Some remains of these dog-spits can be found in Bristol including Blaise Castle Museum. Private collection / The Stapleton Collection / The Bridgeman Art Library

Fry's Transport and General Workers' Union banner depicts the growing and processing of chocolate and sugar. Chocolate beans and sugar cane decorate the picture. Courtesy Bristol Museums, Galleries & Archives

Children enjoying ice-cream from a Verrecchia van in Romney Avenue, Lockleaze c.1960.
Photograph © Peter Dainton

The ancient tradition of wassailing, to wake the fruit trees from the winter, is still practiced at the Horfield Organic Community Orchard. Photograph © Jamie Carstairs

Bristol holds several regular farmers' markets around the city where locally-grown produce and artisan foods can be bought. ©Stephen Morris

Delicatessen shops offer tantalising food from all around the world. This one is the famous Bristol Sweetmart in St Mark's Road, Easton. ©Stephen Morris

From city-centre fine-dining to small neighbourhood cafés, Bristol has an almost limitless choice of dishes.
© Stephen Morris

PLANTATION'S OPENING TIMES

CLOSED SUNDAY – TUESDAY

OPEN WEDNESDAY –
SATURDAY FROM 6PM

Beverley Forbes created the
Plantation Restaurant in the
Gloucester Road in 2003.
The menu is full of authentic
Jamaican dishes including
several different ways of
serving callaloo.
© Stephen Morris

Gas of Delight

In the days when science and literature were closely linked, Bristol attracted both scientists and poets. In 1793, Dr Thomas Beddoes came to Bristol to establish a tuberculosis clinic and also his 'Pneumatic Institution', where he was attempting to prove that inhaling oxygen, hydrogen and other gases could help serious chest diseases, even consumption. He set up in Dowry Square, Hotwells, where many wealthy patients sought cures for their 'distempers'.

News of Beddoes' gas experiments quickly spread and the literary gang flocked down to Dowry Square to try the 'thrill of experiment'. Southey, Coleridge and Lovell all breathed from the bag in which the 'laughing gas' was kept. Cottle described one young lady behaving in a very unladylike fashion: 'she raced downstairs into the Square, leapt over a large dog, and had to be pounced on by a couple of gentlemen'. Their intoxicated experiences with the gas made Southey exclaim: 'I am sure the air in heaven must be this wonder-working gas of delight.'

Green and launched into a 'wild summer of scheming and romance'. Lovell, Southey and Coleridge all married one of the Fricker sisters – high-spirited, dashing girls who were also caught up in the Pantisocratic whirlwind. Their widowed mother kept a dress shop in Bristol and they were always beautifully clothed. Coleridge read widely, studied hard and borrowed liberally from the Bristol Library on King Street; in order to earn money, he gave lectures at Cottle's bookshop and the Philosophical and Literary Institute. Coleridge's talent for public speaking caused considerable alarm and one newspaper correspondent described the poet's arrival in Bristol as 'like a comet or meteor on the horizon'.

During the period when Wordsworth and his sister were staying at Great George Street, the Pinney brothers invited the Pantisocratists and their wives to dinner. It might seem strange for this group of rather wild young literary radicals to have been welcomed in the grand home of John Pinney, one of Bristol's richest and most dedicated slave and sugar traders. But it is unlikely that the elderly Pinney was at home during this time and his liberal-minded sons were free to entertain whom they chose. Coleridge was greedy and passionate about food and enjoyed stimulating conversation whilst gorging on delicious and exotic dishes, often made with ingredients from the West Indies and American colonies. He was inspired by descriptions of life on

Nevis and dreamed of emigrating there with Southey and Wordsworth and 'of making the name of that distant island more illustrious than Cos or Lesbos'. (He later even wrote to old John Pinney requesting permission to live in his house on Nevis.) One wonders what this group of naive idealists thought of the presence of black servants while they enjoyed Pinney's food and hospitality.

Coleridge and Sara Fricker settled down to married life and Coleridge briefly enjoyed domesticity. He was a keen gardener and cook and jotted down recipes in his notebook; he particularly liked apple dumplings and bacon with peas or broad beans, which he grew in his garden. The recipes appear to be designed for large numbers of people and no doubt reflect his dreams of communal life. For ginger ale he lists: 'Six Gallons of Water. Twelve pounds of Sugar, Half a pound of Ginger, Eighteen Lemons and three spoonfuls of Yeast. Boiled together, scum removed and ginger and lemon peel added. Then put in a Gallon Barrel – Close up the Barrel.' Coleridge also wrote out a recipe for a substantial meat and vegetable hotpot, and having cooked it for himself adds the suggestion that it would have been better to season the meat first:

> Take a pound of Beef, Mutton, or Pork; cut it into small pieces; a pint of Peas; four Turnips sliced; six or seven Potatoes cut very small; four or five Onions; put to them three Quarts of Water, let it boil about two hours and a half – then thicken it with a pound of Rice – and boil it a quarter of an hour more – after which season with salt & pepper. N.B. better season it at first – peppering & salting the Meat Etc., –

Family pressures, financial problems and temperamental differences conspired against the poets' fragile dream and Pantisocracy collapsed. Southey and Coleridge became estranged and went off on separate travels and Robert Lovell tragically died in May 1796, leaving Mary a widow with a baby. She moved in with her sister Sara and Coleridge, whose temperament was becoming increasingly erratic. The Coleridges visited the Wordsworths in Dorset and then for a while settled in a sort of community in the Quantocks, where they lived a simple life writing, gardening and dining on 'philosophers' viands of brandy, a loaf of bread, a large piece of local cheese, and lettuces from the garden.' They eventually moved to the Lake District and continued to send work to Cottle in Bristol. Cottle's proudest achievement was to publish the first edition of *Lyrical Ballads*, a collection of early poems by Wordsworth and Coleridge including *Lines Written above Tintern Abbey* and *The Rime of the Ancient Mariner*. By the end of the century, everyone except Cottle had gone from Bristol. Robert Southey lived in London and was made Poet Laureate in 1813 (and was succeeded on his death by Wordsworth). Southey was Bristol's first successful poet, yet Chatterton's name is more famous, and Joseph Cottle's bookshop and his publishing achievements are largely forgotten. The city appears not to have taken much pride in its brief literary associations with the English Romantic Poets. In his first satirical poem, *English Bards and Scotch Reviewers*, a young Lord Byron, then a Cambridge undergraduate, poured unmerciful ridicule on various literary figures including the so-called 'Lakeland Poets' Wordsworth, Southey, Shelley and Coleridge. He even mocked the wretched Cottle in Bristol as he struggled to publish the poets' works:

> Your turtle-feeder's verse must needs be flat,
> Though Bristol bloat him with the verdant fat;
> If Commerce fills the purse, she clogs the brain,
> And Amos Cottle strikes the lyre in vain.
> In him an author's luckless lot behold,
> Condemn'd to make the books which once he sold.

Byron reserved particular ire for the Bristolian passion for turtle meat – and also for sherry; in the same poem he states:

> Too much in turtle Bristol's sons delight,
> Too much o'er bowls of Rack prolong the night.

MODERN TIMES, MODERN FOODS

The nineteenth century, with its increasing modernisation and rapidly developing new ideas, brought fresh things to Bristol's kitchens, highlighting issues from the place of women and the role of mechanisation to new transport networks. On this food journey, Bristol contributed some exceptional individuals, creative family businesses and helpful inventions.

BRISTOL HOSTESSES

When Ellen Sharples stepped ashore in Bristol in June 1811, she was returning from America as a widow with two teenage children and an uncertain future. She was determined to make the best of things for her family. Fortunately they had not been left financially destitute; there was a house waiting in Hotwells, plus a boxful of glowing testimonials for the little family business to build on.

Middle-class women in nineteenth-century Britain were traditionally quietly respectable homemakers, mothers and hostesses, more concerned with running the home and supporting their men than pursuing a career. There were some women, however, who responded to unusual challenges in their lives with great skill and intelligence.

Ellen and her husband James had spent five years travelling in America, making their living by executing miniature portraits for the rich and famous. Their children Rolinda and James, who showed precocious artistic talent, mixed paints, prepared paper and made copies of their parents' work, which were sold profitably. In the age before photography, small, affordable portraits were hugely popular as family mementoes. The family's reputation for accurate portraits and fine copies allowed them to build a successful practice and a modest fortune. America proved all they had dreamed of, as Ellen recorded in her diary:

> There certainly is no country where talents and useful accomplishments are more appreciated nor none where greater hospitality or kindness can be shown to strangers … we live in good style, associating in the First Society.

But, during the extreme cold winter of 1811, James developed heart trouble and died in New York. Shattered by the loss and with impending war between England and America, Ellen took her son and daughter back to England and settled in Hotwells, Bristol, where she established a new portrait business. They continued with pastel portraits of local bigwigs and eminent names such as Robert Southey, then Poet Laureate. But Rolinda, now in her twenties, was moving toward quite a different style of painting. She abandoned miniatures in favour of large narrative oil paintings which portrayed actual places, events and people in Bristol at that time. From the window of their house on Vincent Parade they could see ships sailing down the Avon filled with goods and emigrants leaving for America. They inspected Brunel's drawings and bought shares in his proposed suspension bridge, rambled among the woods and rocks around the gorge, shopped in the markets and went to the races on Durdham Down. They attended concerts and plays and observed high society taking the waters at Hotwell springs or partying at the Assembly Rooms. One of Rolinda's first paintings, *The Cloak-Room, Clifton Assembly Rooms* (1817), features miniature portraits of her friends and society clients as well as herself and her mother dressed up in their best party gowns and hairdos and preparing for an evening's entertainment.

The painting is such an accurate portrayal of provincial genteel society in the Regency era that it has often been used to illustrate the world of Jane Austen. The new Bristol Assembly Room and Hotel in the Mall (now the Clifton Club) was opened in 1811 and, with its fine ballroom, soon became the focal point for Clifton society's social life. This 'spacious and elegant' building, claimed a Bristol guide, 'contained a noble reception saloon and tea room, with convenient lobbies, a billiard room etc' and 'every accommodation for both families and individuals, even to sets of apartments/drawing rooms, a coffee room, a shop for pastry and confectionery, with an adjoining room for soups, fruits and ices; hot, cold and vapour baths'. Many of Rolinda's paintings depict people and events with humour and social accuracy and offer a lively portrayal of Bristol life during the 25 years she lived there. For example, milling crowds on Durdham Down enjoy themselves in *The Clifton Race Course* and cheerful holidaymakers queue to cross the river at Rownham in *Taking the Ferry*. Another, darker side to Bristol also attracted Rolinda's interest, and she painted a number of dramatic records of events during the 1820s and 1830s. *The Stoppage at the Bank* (1825) was produced at a time of many bank failures and bankruptcies. It featured the terrible scene in Corn Street on the day when a bank closed and many Bristolians believed they were ruined. *The Trial of Colonel Brereton after the Bristol Riots* was based on the Bristol Reform riots of 1831, when rioters, drunk on wine plundered from the Mansion House cellars, tore through Bristol city centre, burning and looting. Rolinda had herself witnessed the terrifying events and recorded in her diary:

> There was something awful in the flames, and the perfect stillness, not a bell was rung in any of the churches, as is usual in accidental fires. After an almost sleepless night of alarm, sometimes watching the inflamed sky from the back of the house, sometimes fancying the voices of the mob approaching, and a thousand imaginary fears, morning at length dawned. Small groups of anxious inquirers were almost at every door, strangers accosted one another without the ceremony of intro-duction; terror and dismay were depicted on every countenance.

Rather than paint the terrible scenes of rioting, Rolinda had chosen to depict the trial of Colonel Brereton, commander of the local troops, who, out of sympathy for the people's cause, refused to fire on the rioters. He was subse-quently court-martialled for his failure to stop the riot, but on the second day of the trial, he committed suicide. This large painting featured over a hundred individual faces, including the artist and her mother plus almost every high-ranking member of Bristol society.

Rolinda's mother, Ellen, had meanwhile given up her own art and thrown herself wholeheartedly into promoting her daughter's work. An independent-minded woman, professional artist and devoted mother, Ellen was ambitious to promote Rolinda, whose career as a female artist in the first decades of the nineteenth century was both unusual and an impressive achievement. The Bristol-born portraitist, Sir Thomas Lawrence, president of the Royal Acad-emy in London, encouraged Rolinda to exhibit in the capital. But Ellen knew that real success meant they would have to court wealthy and influential members of Bristol and London society, attending a social-cultural round that included not just balls, concerts, plays, art exhibitions and lectures, but also, of course, teas and dinners. Ellen realised she would need to hold intimate soirées and small dinner parties for potential patrons – and to do this she would have to polish up her skills as a hostess.

Now that she had a permanent home in fashionable Hotwells, Ellen would certainly have employed a maid and a cook, but, as was common in those days, she controlled the food purchases, planned the menus and instructed her cook. Like many educated ladies of the time, Ellen began to keep a small notebook into which she wrote instructions for economic house-keeping, cooking and preserving advice, and recipes. Fortunately, this little book has survived and it gives tantalising clues about cooking in a provincial, middle-class nineteenth-century kitchen.

There are several surprises in Ellen's cookbook. Almost all the recipes and advice are old-fashioned and have clearly been copied from cookery and household-management books from a much earlier period. The probable reason for this is that war and the harsh economic climate of this time meant that almost no new cookery books were being published. Housewives were still reading reprints of the many popular books that first appeared in the late eighteenth century – some 30 years earlier. Even these recipes sometimes seem rather outdated for their time, and this is because the authors of these books notoriously copied from even earlier cookbooks. Ellen only refers to the name of one cook, John Farley. Formerly principal cook at the London Tavern in the capital's Bishopsgate, Farley published *The London Art of Cookery and Domestic Housekeeper's Complete Assistant* in 1783. Yet nearly all the recipes and observations in Farley's book were lifted from earlier publications such as *The Experienced English Housekeeper* (1743), which was compiled by Elizabeth Raffald, a retired housekeeper who ran a shop in Manchester selling baked products, 'made dishes' and confectionery. She claimed that her recipes and methods, written in plain, simple English, were aimed at the middle-class mistress of the house who could copy out instructions and recipes and hand them to her cook. She too had copied many of her recipes from Hannah Glasse, who had also been in service and who wrote her best-selling *The Art of Cookery* just three years earlier. Several of Glasse's recipes were, in turn, 'borrowed' from Hannah Woolley's 1661 edition of *The Lady's Companion*. Woolley had reworked some even earlier recipes, intended for upper-class households, into a practical, more frugal format for women in service as well as those living in towns, where shop-purchased food was more expensive and self-sufficiency impossible.

In this game of culinary 'Chinese Whispers', one wonders how all these recipes, copied and recopied so many times, could still be cookable and edible. Perhaps it was because the writers did at least test and even improve them a little each time. It is impossible to say accurately which of these books Ellen was copying from, and it probably did not matter at all to Ellen anyway. Though, given her interest in women's education and achievements, it seems odd to copy the pirated efforts of a male chef rather than those of experienced female housekeepers, cooks and mistresses of the home. Perhaps, when she first returned from America intent on setting up a home in fashionable society, a friend had given Ellen the newly printed 1811 edition of John Farley's 28-year-old book.

There does not seem to be any order or structure in Ellen's little exercise book, and one can imagine her taking it up now and then to copy something that attracted her interest or which she thought might impress her guests.

There are several lists of dishes but few complete recipes and plenty of 'Observations' and advice on how to avoid mistakes and the best method to achieve perfect results. Food preserving was of particular concern in Ellen's frugal household. She mentions portable soup – a fairly recent discovery whereby soups or stocks could be reduced down to a small dry block and later reconstituted with water. But older methods of preserving were also still being used, such as potting shrimps to keep them under thick layers of fat or clarified butter and preserving fruit and vegetables. The latter included keeping mushrooms, cucumbers, cranberries and damsons in bottles filled with salt water, or using a vinegar pickle – as in 'Pickled Codlins in vine leaves' and kidney beans 'young and small'. Ellen notes severe warnings about the perils of storing pickles in pottery with lead glazes and of making pickles with vinegar in inadequately tinned copper pans (copper poisoning can be fatal). To prevent mould, she writes: 'dip best writing paper in Brandy and lay it close to your sweetmeats and keep in a cool, dry place'.

Cooking meat was very much a priority and several pages are filled with dishes of minced, hashed, roasted and stewed meats such as roast beef, stewed venison, neck of mutton and veal, calf's head hash, fricassees of rabbit, jugged hare, Scotch Collops (thin rashers of meat) with 'catchup' (ketchup – usually of mushrooms) and 'Pyes' (pies) filled with pigeon, larks, woodcock or snipe. There are recipes for collared meat – a process involving cooked and pickled/marinated meat which is then rolled and tied, pressed, cooled and cut into slices for eating. Ellen found one particularly illuminating observation: 'A cook cannot be guilty of a greater error than to let any kind of meat boil fast, it hardens the outside before the inside is warm, & discolours it, especially veal.'

Although Ellen ran a careful household, she wanted to impress and, like

Collared Beef

This recipe comes from *The Cookbook of Unknown Ladies*, whose authorship is uncertain and which seems to contain recipes from the 1700s and 1800s.

Take a plate of beef & bone it & put it in spring water for four & twenty hours. Then, take it out & dry it. Season it with pepper, salt, mace & 2 penny worth of salt peter & 1 pint of claret. Lay it all night in these & get a great deal of sweet

COLLARED BEEF.

herbs, cut them small & lay them on the inside of the beef & bind it up very hard with tape & put it in yr pan for baking with 2 unnions. You may cover it or not. If it be not very large, it will take 5 hours baking.

many in her position, she resorted to a little cheating. The constant need for the less well-off to be able to keep up appearances led to all kinds of recipes for ingenious cheats and mock dishes – anything from melon cut to look like mangoes to 'mock' venison. Everyone wanted venison but few could obtain it, so Ellen's recipe for Mock Venison Pasty hopefully made a convincingly delicious and cheap alternative to serve at a dinner:

> Take shoulder of mutton, lay it in red port all night and bake first in a coarse paste. Then make a puff paste and bake the mix in this as you would a venison pasty.

Fresh turtle was still a sought-after dish which presented special problems. One could substitute turtle with beef or mutton – but really the authentic thing was still expected. Ellen copied out advice on slaughtering and 'dressing' (cooking) a monster turtle weighing 30 lb: 'Kill the night before, cut off the head and let it bleed 2 or 3 hours and stew with mace, nutmeg, sweet marjoram parsley and 3 glasses of Madeira for about 3 hours.' It seems hard to imagine how anyone working in a small kitchen in Hotwells would be capable of preparing a live turtle in this way, or indeed that fresh, slaughtered turtle was still available by the mid 1800s – but apparently it was: 'To butcher a turtle you start by chopping off the turtle's head. Be careful because the head will still bite even after it is removed from the body and the body will still crawl away after the head is removed. Turtles don't die right away.' Perhaps Ellen's experiences in America gave her a strong constitution when it came to slaughtering, as she also includes a recipe for boiled turkey with oyster sauce: 'Starve the Turkey for a day or two before you kill it.'

Ellen also copied out some useful advice for cake making – 'Be sure to get everything ready beforehand' – along with recipes for cakes to serve guests at afternoon teas, which include: seed cake, plum cake, macaroons with almonds, Ratafia cakes, Shrewsbury cakes, Barbadoes Jumballo (like macaroons), gingerbread and drop biscuits. There are also several useful 'Observations of Pyes', such as 'A raised pye should have a quick oven and well closed up, or your pye will fall in the sides. It should have no water put in till the minute it goes in the oven as it makes the crust sag and is a great hazard of the pye-making.' A 'Thatched House Pye' is an unusual recipe for a novelty, conversation-piece pie: in a deep earthenware dish put three or four pigeon on their sides, with a thick paste made with crushed vermicelli covering them to look like thatch. 'It is a pretty idea for a large dinner.'

Homemade wines were regularly produced in the Sharples' kitchen, including wine made from raisins, ginger, gooseberry, blackberry, redcurrant, cowslip and lemon balm. Ellen noted: 'Wine is a very necessary thing in most families, and is often spoiled through mismanagement. It is important to be clear about standing, bottling, corking etc.' Other popular drinks in the Sharples household were Sack Posset, hot chocolate, barley gruel, mulled wine and various kinds of sherbets.

There are the inevitable 'Observations on puddings' such as trifles, tarts, custards, cheesecakes, syllabubs, fritters and pancakes, and a rice pudding made with bread, suet, milk, lemon rind, eggs, cinnamon and nutmeg – but no rice! This 'Transparent Pudding' sounds intriguing:

> Beat 8 eggs very well, & put them in a pan, with half a pound of butter and the same weight of loaf sugar, beat fine with a little grated nutmeg. Set it on the fire and keep stirring it till it thickens like buttered eggs, then set it in a bason [sic] to cool. Roll out a rich stiff paste very thin, lay it around the edge of a china dish, then pour in the pudding, and bake it in a warm oven half an hour, it will come out light & clear. It is a pretty pudding for a corner for dinner, and a middle for supper.

This reference to the position of a dish on the table is particularly interesting because it was around this time that the customary seating and serving arrangements for dinner parties were changing. The old-fashioned service *à la Française*, where all the food was displayed on the table at once, had been displaced by service *à la Russe*, where guests were served each course individually. This meant that food had not been sitting around getting cold and congealed and everyone had a chance to choose what and how much they wished to put on their plate.

Towards the end of the little book, Ellen's daughter Rolinda began copying her own snippets of advice, plus a few recipes which perhaps appealed more to her artist's sense of colour and drama than taste: 'To pot hare or other meat to look like a plum cake', she wrote, and 'How to make a yellow pickle the East India Way'. But scattered among her food entries are some very different sorts of recipes. Inserted between 'New College Pudding' and 'How to prevent hung game from going mouldy', Rolinda has written up some highly technical instructions for mixing paint: 'Mix your lamp black with spirits and water and warm it into a crucible and burn it till it is almost red hot. It must not be put in too thin'; and 'Good Prussian Blue' should made be made by 'grinding it with a small quantity of unburnt lamp black and white'.

Rolinda was elected an honorary member of the Society of British Artists, the highest honour possible for a woman artist at that time, and she continued to exhibit at the London Royal Academy. But her career was tragically cut short when, in 1838, she died of breast cancer at the age of 45. A year and a half later her brother James also died, of tuberculosis. Ellen was grief-stricken by the loss of both beloved children: 'a dark, blighting cloud suddenly threw its sombre shadow over all', she wrote to a friend. Ellen lived on alone in Bristol supporting women's education, especially in art. When she died in 1849, aged 80, she bequeathed her considerable estate and the family art collection to the founding of the Bristol Academy for the Promotion of Fine Arts – now the Royal West of England Academy.

Most Victorian women, even those with a good education, were still expected to carry out traditional domestic duties and Florence Walwyn, the youngest unmarried daughter of a genteel family living in Sion Hill, Clifton, had responsibility for the family meals. Like Ellen Sharples, Florence kept a book of recipes copied from cookery books. Many of her collected recipes were given to her by members of the family's large circle of friends, and they illustrate a wide range of tastes and choices, from old English to Empire. Cooking at home was becoming increasingly influenced by wider foreign travel and by the eating experiences of families working for the British East India Company or in Government posts around the Empire.

Dr Symonds, a lecturer at the Bristol Medical School, gave Florence a recipe for a solid-sounding steak and oyster pudding with macaroni, boiled in a cloth; Methodist minister John W. Cowell contributed a recipe for a spicy Anglo-Indian soup called Mulaga-Tawny Soup – really a kind of curried-chicken-in-the-pot, then new to England from the East Indies. Dr William Kitchiner, in *The Cook's Oracle* (1817), attacked its colourful name:

> This outlandish word is pasted on the windows of our Coffee Houses and often excites John Bull to walk in and taste. The more familiar word Curry Soup would perhaps not have sufficient charms or novelty to seduce him from his much loved Mock Turtle.

The Tyndall family of Royal Fort gave Florence numerous recipes, such as one for baked 'Belvidere Pudding', made with green gooseberries and Naples biscuits. Mrs Smart, on returning from her travels, produced instructions for making Bobotie, a mild curry dish from South Africa using pounded meat or fish, flavoured with spices favoured by Cape Malay cooks such as tamarind, cumin and green ginger. It was topped with beaten egg yolks in milk and baked, then decorated with apricots and almonds and served with yellow rice. Mrs Smart writes that Bobotie is 'very good either for breakfast or dinner … It may be made in a small pie dish but looks much prettier in small china coffee cups'.

A new generation of college-educated women was also attempting to

Dr Kitchiner's Original Recipe for Mulligatawny Soup

Take two quarts of water and a nice fowl or chicken. Then put in the following ingredients:

A large white onion; I large chilli (the pods from which the cayenne pepper is made); 2 teaspoons pounded ginger; the same of curry stuff; 1 teaspoon turmeric, and ½ dram black pepper.

Boil all these for half an hour and then fry some small onions and put them in. Season it with salt, and serve it in a tureen.

Some Nineteenth-Century Favourites

Florence Walwyn's Filets de soles à l'Orlie

Take the skin off the soles. Cut off the slices; soak them for 2 hours in lemon juice with parsley, slices of onion or shallots, salt and pepper. Drain them on a clean towel.

Put them in flour; egg and crumb and fry and serve with tomato sauce or sharp sauce. (Whiting may be dressed in the same way)

Dr Symond's Steak and Vegetable Pudding

Prepare steaks or slices of mutton by taking off all the fat & gristle. Have a small quantity of onion chopped fine; a little celery cut into pieces; some macaroni previously cooked and a doz of oysters. Mix the vegetables, macaroni and oysters together with pepper and salt. Put a layer of the vegetables etc at the bottom of an upright earthenware vessel; then a layer of meat; then the vegetables; and so on till all is put in. Add 2 tablespoons of good stock.

Have ready a flour and water crust to put over the vessel. Tie it up in a cloth and put it into a saucepan with boiling water, taking care that the water does not come above 2 or 3 inches from the bottom of the basin. Stew gently for 4 hours.

Traditional College Pudding

This is a winter-warmer suet pudding which some have likened to that favourite steamed pudding, Spotted Dick. College Pudding is said to have come from Cambridge, served to students in college halls. Both Ellen Sharples and Mary Paley Marshall would have made a version of it. The earliest known recipe is from 1617. There are several Victorian and later versions; some involve steaming, some involve shallow frying, but the Beeton version offered below – which is a good way to use up stale bread – involves deep-fat frying the puddings, rather like dough-nuts.

'A nice fowl or chicken' for Dr Kitchiner's Mulligatawny Soup from Taylor's game and poultry shop, St Nicholas Street ('established 1787')

Mrs Beeton's College Pudding

1 pint of bread crumbs, 6 oz. of finely-chopped suet, ¼ lb. of currants, a few thin slices of candied peel, 3 oz. of sugar, ¼ nutmeg, 3 eggs, 4 tablespoonfuls of brandy.

Put the bread crumbs into a basin; add the suet, currants, candied peel, sugar, and nutmeg, grated, and stir these ingredients until they are thoroughly mixed.

Beat up the eggs, moisten the pudding with these, and put in the brandy; beat well for a few minutes, then form the mixture into round balls or egg-shaped pieces; fry these in hot butter or lard, letting them stew in it until thoroughly done, and turn them two or three times, till of a fine light brown; drain them on a piece of blotting-paper before the fire; dish, and serve with wine sauce.

Bristol's Mothering Bun

Mothering Bun is a speciality of Bristol, still made by several bakers on the Saturday immediately preceding Mothering Sunday (mid Lent Sunday). The Lenten fast was briefly relaxed so that these rich buns could be enjoyed – rather like the tradition of eating a Simnel Cake. Simnel Cake is much richer and more elaborate; Mothering Buns are small and rather plain. Until recently there was a baker in Bristol called John Williams who claimed that, by the beginning of the twentieth century, Mothering Buns were coated with caraway or aniseed comfits, like Bath Buns, in place of the hundreds-and-thousands which are now used.

A plain dough is made with flour, fat and sugar in the proportions 10:1:1. A ferment works for about 30 minutes at 32°C. The fat – either lard or butter – is rubbed into the flour and sugar and a little salt and the ferment are added. After fermentation, it is knocked back and kneaded again. It is baked at 22°C for 20 minutes. The tops are given a plain icing, followed immediately by dipping in a dish of hundreds-and-thousands.

(Recipe courtesy of Laura Mason)

combine a professional life with domesticity. Mary Paley Marshall, wife of Alfred Marshall, the famous economist, recalled 'delightful' dinner parties she had hosted in honour of Bristol College Council meetings in the 1870s. Mary was herself a first-rate economist and, despite the fact that women at that time had no right to a degree, she passed the Cambridge exams in political economy and logic with distinction. In 1876, Alfred Marshall was appointed the first Principal, and Professor of Political Economy, of the new University College in Bristol. Mary did not, however, settle down to become a dutiful academic's wife. Instead she taught female students at the college, which was the first to experiment in co-education (though her fee was deducted from her husband's salary), and also gave her husband's lectures when he later fell ill.

Mary and Alfred Marshall lived in a modest house in Clifton, where they gave regular dinner parties for around 12 people. Mary enjoyed a long relationship with her cook Sarah, one of 13 children of a Plymouth Brethren farm labourer from Somerset. Sarah's father earned 11 shillings per week, and Sarah told Mary of the 'shocking bread and rotten potatoes on which they were fed'. Sarah was an excellent cook who 'loved doing the dinners; she ran the whole concern and would lie awake at nights considering the menus for the day'. Mary particularly enjoyed stimulating gatherings at the table and she became a member of a Ladies Dining Society where 10 or 12 dined in one another's houses once or twice a term, 'the husbands either dining at their colleges or having a solitary meal in their studies'. The hostess not only provided a good dinner (though champagne was not allowed) but also a suitable topic of conversation; 'we had some good talks', Mary recalled. She was amused by the gentlemen academics, who, while returning home from a dinner, instead of 'high talk' did nothing but discuss the sauces they had had for dinner. But 'the favourite topic, after food, was sex'. During their five years in Bristol, the Marshalls made many close friends, including Albert and Lewis Fry, who worked tirelessly to set up the University, using their wealth from the chocolate business. Unfortunately, Mary's husband adopted an increasingly reactionary view that a woman's place was in the home. Despite her own belief in the need for women to gain economic independence through education, Mary gave up teaching to devote herself to her husband as he became increasingly infirm.

KEEPING IT IN THE FAMILY

Several Bristol-linked family businesses played pioneering roles in promoting important foods in nineteenth-century Bristol.

FLOUR

Henry Jones was a Monmouth baker who came to Bristol in 1803 and opened a bakery in Broadmead. It was not the best time to be selling bread and his business struggled through a tough period of grain shortages. He saw great hardship among his customers and then in 1815, to make matters worse, when the Napoleonic Wars had finally come to an end, the Government introduced the Corn Laws. These were meant to protect British agriculture by preventing the importation of foreign grain, but a lack of imported corn on top of four successive years of bad harvests produced terrible shortages, and harsh measures to conserve corn had to be taken. In Bristol, the distillation of corn for alcohol was banned; the manufacture of cornstarch was suspended; millers were prohibited from producing fine flour; and bakers were only permitted to make brown bread and forbidden to reheat and sell stale bread (one Bristol baker was fined £19s 10d for infringing the Stale Bread Laws). The mayor of Bristol nobly announced that the Mansion House dinners would be restricted to a single course; the serving of bread at 'afternoon tea' would be given up; pastry of every kind tabooed from the tables of the rich; wearers of hair-powder had to use substitutes for flour or drop the practice altogether; poultices at public institutions were ordered to be made of linseed or turnips; and persons in receipt of relief from the poor laws were forbidden to keep dogs (though what this last rule had to do with flour consumption is a mystery).

History seemed to be repeating itself, and once again there were food riots in Bristol and attacks on food stalls in the city markets. Hungry country people flocked to the city hoping for food and were turned away. As a result of the enclosing of land in the eighteenth century, many thousands of rural workers and their families had lost their small vegetable plots, even their homes. In desperation, they trekked to the slum-filled cities to seek work in the factories being set up. If they were lucky to find a job, an urban newcomer might be able to afford a little bit of bacon once a week, but potatoes and mostly bread or porridge were their daily staple. Strong tea made from reboiled leaves, which gave an illusion of warmth and fullness, was the main comfort. Substitute flour was made from rice, oats, barley, rye and peas, and some housewives were reported to be making loaves from potatoes. Bristol's authorities struggled to cope: huge quantities of potatoes were imported from Ireland and fishing fleets were fitted out with additional boats, with bounties paid for extra catches of fish. The rich did rally round and make contributions towards relief efforts, such as the Bristol Flour and Bread Concern, a system of cooperative trading in flour. But as supplies diminished, the price of corn and wheat continued to rise. Inevitably it was the poorest, for whom bread was the great staple, who were hardest hit.

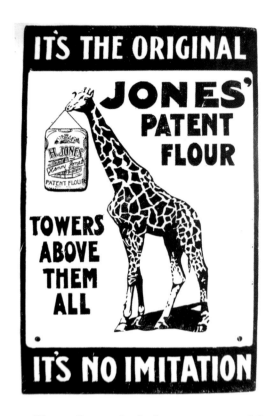

Henry Jones the baker was meanwhile experimenting with a new process for baking without yeast. For centuries, yeast had been used for baking bread and brewing beer but its greatest drawback was that it did not keep well and many housewives found it tricky to use. In 1845, Jones took out a patent for a revolutionary new baking ingredient; he called it self-raising flour.

Jones was not just an inventive baker, he was also a shrewd businessman, and his flour was soon selling in huge quantities around the country. A clever salesman, he sent a case of his flour to the Duke of Beaufort at Badminton and received a reply from the duke's chief cook requesting two more cases 'of your excellent flour'. One case was to be sent on to the head chef of the Royal Yacht; 'By this means Her Majesty is sure to eat Bread made from your Flour.' The strategy worked, and within six months Henry Jones had received a Royal Warrant and was appointed purveyor of patent flour and biscuits to Queen Victoria. Jones' Bristol Flour business was fully established, with orders flooding in from influential customers countrywide. He became very wealthy and mixed with society, riding to hounds and enjoying country pursuits with the gentry. With his flair for clever marketing, Jones continued to lead the field from his factory in Broadmead. The symbol on his packets of flour was a giraffe with the slogan, 'Towers above them all'. His most appealing advertisement posed the question:

Why is Jones' patent flour like the sun? Because they are both original and self-raising and their beneficial effects are alike appreciated in the palace and the cottage.

But Henry Jones had more ambitious plans still. He knew that in those days, new inventions, such as recent developments with canned and dehydrated foods, could only be really successful if they were accepted by the army and navy, leading to bulk orders. There had always been huge problems in providing soldiers and seamen with fresh food, especially bread. New methods of preserving food for long voyages at sea and for campaigns far from supply lines were desperately needed. Biscuit-making factories in Bristol were still turning out inedible 'hardtack' (tough bread) for seamen, and troops serving in the Crimean War around that time, for example, suffered badly from the lack of fresh bread. The wounded soldiers in hospital ships were especially affected: 'I suppose all English people can imagine the sour bread which is all that is to be had here and the bad butter, too', a nurse in Scutari wrote to *The Times* in 1855; 'A stolen scrape of this is the greatest luxury to a dying man.'

Time and again Henry Jones wrote to the War Office and the Admiralty describing the huge benefits his self-raising flour could offer. Each time he was ignored. He strove to convince them that, although a diet of 'maggots, weevils and mouldy biscuits' may have been tolerated by Nelson's crews, 'only good bread, decently baked, would satisfy the modern seaman'. He took out a patent in America, where he won a gold medal for his new flour and glowing testimonials were published by doctors, medical experts and sea captains who had taken Jones' patent flour on merchant ships and passenger liners. The master of the *Jumma*, sailing in the Indian Ocean, wrote that:

When I asked the steward how it was likely to answer he said it was the best invention that he knew of this many a day. At all events, we had splendid hot rolls for breakfast this morning! I shall take care to let all my friends in Calcutta know of it.

Jones continued to be frustrated by the attitude of the British navy. He visited the Admiralty in London, where he demonstrated his newly invented bread-making machine for use on board ship. Almost a year later he was asked to send the machine to Woolwich for trial on board HMS *Porcupine*. His hopes were high but again were dashed when officials informed him that his machine had been broken up for scrap. Henry - was now so angry that he fired back a reply pointing out that the machine had been built to last for 50 years – and he was at least paid compensation. At last, in May 1849, he received a favourable report in which both flour and machine were pronounced admirable. But, eight days later, an abrupt letter informed Jones that 'their Lordships' had declined to make use of either for the navy. Later, in 1854, Jones was so shocked by newspaper reports of the terrible conditions in the hospitals for sick and wounded soldiers fighting in the Crimea that he was moved to make one more effort. Being convinced, as he said, 'that a grave responsibility would rest upon himself if he did not make this attempt', he sent a pamphlet, plus testimonials and positive dietary reports, including an article in the *Lancet*, to every Member of Parliament.

It was at this time that Alexis Soyer, the famous French chef and food guru, was sent to the Crimea as adviser on catering – having been similarly employed by the Government in Ireland setting up soup kitchens during the famine. Working closely with nursing pioneer Florence Nightingale, Soyer reorganised the cooking of food for sick and injured troops. English soldiers had a daily ration of one pound of salt meat (which had to be soaked in water for some hours before it could be cooked) and one pound of tough hardtack, plus an allowance of coffee, salt, sugar and water, all of which they had to carry (and they cooked for themselves). The lack of fruit or vegetables meant most of them suffered from scurvy and their sore, scorbutic gums could not chew the hard bread. Soyer set up 'floating bakeries' on two ships anchored in Balaklava harbour where he created his 'bread biscuit', said to be very palatable when dunked in soup or tea. He was an admirer of Jones' self-raising flour and believed that good bread, made with Jones' flour, was an essential and achievable part of a good diet. By introducing his own newly invented field stove, plus a French formula for pressed, dried vegetables and Henry Jones' self-raising flour, Alexis Soyer transformed the catering and health of Englishmen fighting in the Crimea.

Self-raising flour revolutionised Victorian cooking, and by the time Henry Jones' patent had ended, several other manufactures had adopted the flour and turned baking into a highly competitive industry. Succeeding generations of the Jones family continued to expand, producing biscuits and several varieties of flour. The company eventually moved out of its premises in Broadmead to Bedminster. A long tradition of good working relations between employer and employees was a hallmark of the company.

Henry Jones was just one of the successful food pioneers in Victorian Bristol to develop and patent modern ideas for food and drink. Gradually life improved, with more industry, more employment and more food on the table.

The growth of Britain's Empire and its expansion, powered by the Industrial Revolution, encouraged numerous hardworking business families to develop new ideas and profit by them. Most such businesses emerged from generations of one family that had first set up a small concern in the previous century. In 1847, two years after Henry Jones was awarded a patent for self-raising flour, Joseph Fry II took out a patent for the first chocolate bar.

CHOCOLATE

Grandfather Fry was a Quaker who set up his apothecary business in Bristol in 1753. At that time chocolate was thought to be medicinal, so it made sense for an apothecary, who was both doctor and chemist, to prescribe and sell it. Some time earlier, another apothecary called Walter Churchman had devised a method of grinding the cocoa beans to make a smoother drink and was granted a patent in 1728. After Churchman's death, Fry bought the patent and continued to improve the process. Chocolate was a popular drink enjoyed by gentlemen in coffee houses and also by ladies at home in their parlour. But it was nothing like the sweet, hot chocolate enjoyed today; the drink that Samuel Pepys had described was thick, gritty and bitter-tasting, more like coffee. No wonder black pepper, cinnamon or chillies were often added to improve the flavour.

Fry was a wise businessman and clever inventor who expanded his interests in several directions. He set up a typesetting firm in London and designed a new typeface still used today called Fry's Baskerville. He ran alkali works in both London and Bristol, which rendered animal fats to produce tallow for soap and candles, and owned several other business enterprises, including one involving a new process in porcelain production which he sold to Richard Champion's porcelain works in Bristol. When Fry died in 1787 the older sons took over the printing, type-founding, chemical and porcelain interests. The youngest, Joseph Storrs Fry, who was then aged 20, joined his mother running the chocolate business and on her death took full control. He married Ann, a Quaker minister who, like Joseph's niece, the famous Elizabeth Fry, was concerned with prison reform.

Joseph Storrs Fry was keen to develop his father's chocolate-processing methods further by adapting the latest technology. He installed the newly invented Watt steam engine in his factory in Union Street and used it to grind cocoa beans more efficiently – and obtained a patent for his method. A London newspaper, impressed with the scale of Fry's production, reported that

> for the trifling object of grinding chocolate … in the recently erected factory … Either the consumption of this little article must far exceed our ideas or, which we think much more likely, a very large proportion

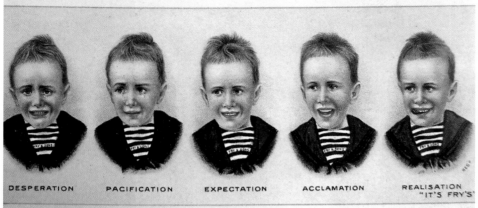

It is said that the American photographer of this famous advertisement for Fry's 'Five Boys' chocolate bar used his son as the model and made him cry before rewarding him with the chocolate. Courtesy Bristol Museums, Galleries and Archives

of what is drunk in this little kingdom must be made by him [Fry]. In 1800, Joseph Storrs Fry moved to a grand house in the popular Quaker community at Frenchay, where his three sons grew up and eventually joined him in the chocolate business. As one of the young Fry boys recalled, the factory in Union Street was still comparatively modest, with 16 employees: 'There was a small back-yard, and beyond a small steam-engine and grinding mills, and at the side of our house a counting-house and a packing-house, with windows halfway up blocked to prevent passersby looking in.' One old man packed boxes of chocolate which 'from time to time' were sent to London by canal; there was a woman 'who was always sitting and pasting on labels' and an old clerk who did accounts at a raised desk by the door. 'So far as I recollect no change ever occurred in this routine of peaceful business.' When Storrs Fry died in 1835, he left the chocolate business to his sons, who quickly diversified into other areas such as coal mining, breweries, railways and transport. Meanwhile, the 'peaceful' but thriving chocolate business was about to grow into something much bigger.

It was the eldest son, Joseph Fry II, who, by harnessing the latest industrialised processes, pushed chocolate production forward into a major enterprise. He planned to make chocolate into something you could eat as well as drink.

Although his father had made chocolate lozenges, no one had thought of making chocolate into a solid sweetmeat. In 1847, he produced the first solid chocolate bar, which he called *chocolat délicieux à manger* (French-sounding food had a considerable cachet at this time). The bar was made with a mixture of cocoa powder and sugar, plus some melted cocoa butter that had been extracted from the beans (until then the cocoa butter or paste was considered a waste product). The result could be poured into a mould, cooled and turned out as a solid bar of chocolate. Later, Joseph filled the centres of chocolate bars with mint fondue and called them Fry's Cream Sticks, Cream Batons or tablets, and finally Fry's Chocolate Cream, which can still be bought today. The other best-selling chocolates were Five Boys chocolate bar, Fry's Peppermint Cream and Fry's Turkish Delight.

Like Henry Jones and his self-raising flour, Joseph Fry II knew the huge value of obtaining a contract to be sole suppliers of chocolate to the Royal Navy. Fortunately, he was more successful than Jones. The navy at that time was trying to wean its sailors from a reliance on grog or rum and chocolate seemed to be a good and healthy alternative. An exclusive deal with the Royal Navy pushed J.S. Fry & Sons of Bristol into its position as the largest chocolate manufacturers in the world. But the Fry dynasty was soon facing serious rivals: two other Quaker families of chocolate makers, Cadbury and Sons of Bournville, Birmingham, and Rowntree of York, were jostling for top position. Cadbury scored a coup in 1866 with a royal patent to supply Queen Victoria. The firm also obtained a new Dutch machine and produced its own patent cocoa powder labelled 'Cadbury's Cocoa Essence', which was an instant hit. Fry's quickly countered with their 'Cocoa Extract', but two years later Cadbury introduced the first 'chocolate box', containing chocolate candies. Cocoa powder was also becoming popular as a flavouring ingredient for cakes, ice-creams and biscuits, and housewives bought packets of Cadbury cocoa powder for cooking at home. By the time of Victoria's Diamond Jubilee in 1897, Cadbury's had surpassed Fry & Sons in total chocolate sales. By the end of the Great War, Fry's had merged with their rival. The giant US food company, Kraft Foods, bought the combined business. Despite promises not to close the factory at Somerdale, Keynsham, production has been moved to Poland and over 400 employees lost their jobs.

SHERRY

There were several famous family dynasties trading in food and drink which prospered over the centuries and changed Bristol's fortunes. One name that is particularly linked with Bristol is Harvey's and its famous sherry. There were once hundreds of local merchants trading in wine but only two, Averys

Wood engraving of Bristol Quay by
David Gentleman for a post-war
Harveys advertisement

(founded 1793) and John Harvey & Sons (founded 1796), are still operating. The Harveys were originally a Cornish family of coastal mariners, but in 1755 they settled in Bristol. The first Harvey was for 12 years master of the massive ship, the *Bristol*, but perished in a storm in the Atlantic along with his wife and the ship's crew. His son Thomas also went to sea and ran ships for a West India merchant bringing sugar and rum into Bristol. In 1805, Thomas met and married Anne Urch, whose brother was a partner in the wine firm of Perry & Urch. When their young sons John and Charles joined the firm, they were sent to learn the wine business from another partner, based in Kidderminster. It is said that at the end of their training, they tossed a coin to see who would stay in Kidderminster and who would return to Bristol. John lost and went home to work in the premises in Denmark Street.

Wine had been imported into Bristol since the twelfth century, and despite wars, piracy and restrictive trade, the port was perfectly situated to trade with Gascony, Iberia and the Mediterranean. For centuries, Bristol continued to be the major wine importer for the whole country. At that time the English liked their wine to be sweet and often added sugar, so Bristol merchants imported sweet wines from Iberia and the more potent sweet, blended and fortified wine from the Andalusian town of Jerez, which was instantly popular. One of the earliest mentions of 'sherris sack', as it was first called, was back in 1577, when *The Bristol Calendar* recorded a cargo arriving into Bristol: 'came from Andoluzia sundre sweete and pleasant seckes in general as by report the like was never knowen'. Elizabethans drank it in huge quantities, and there was great demand from the numerous Bristol inns and taverns, where it 'went down a treat'. In the seventeenth century, sherry, as it came to be called, was more commonly enjoyed during meals at home.

Meanwhile, deep underground in their cellars, Bristol wine merchants began experimenting with blending and maturing imported Spanish wines, until they came up with a winning formula and called it Bristol Milk. In its earliest days, people believed in its health-giving qualities. In 1662, Thomas

Harvey's sherry/wine barrels being
unloaded in the docks, 1930s.
Picture source unknown

Fuller wrote in his *Worthies of England* that 'some will have it called Milk
because, where in some places nurses give new-born babes pap and other
water and sugar, such Wine is the first moisture given to Infants in this City
[Bristol]'. In 1750, a Bristol doctor in Castle Street treated patients suffering
from dropsy with Bristol Milk, and midwives prescribed it for mothers after
childbirth. It was claimed that, during the Civil War, the Bristol garrison, 'being
well-furnished with Bristol Milk' and its energy-giving properties, should have
held out against the Royalists forces, who, after taking the city, drank the lot
themselves. Despite the Napoleonic Wars and the recession which followed,
causing many bankruptcies in Bristol, numerous small wine firms managed
to survive and prosper. By the mid nineteenth century, Bristol was importing
the lion's share of Spanish sherry and re-exporting its own blends around the
world. Over the centuries, numerous eminent visitors to Bristol enthusiastically
endorsed Bristol Milk; when the Prince of Wales visited in 1901 and tasted
Bristol Cream, he joked that Bristol must have 'dam' fine cows'.

By 1834, John Harvey was a prosperous partner in the firm. He lived with
his wife, four sons and four daughters over the shop in Denmark Street until
he was rich enough to buy a big house in Redland Park. He was a hard-work-
ing, cultivated man who loved music and fine things. He took the family to
London to see the Great Exhibition in 1851, where he bought a set of fine
engraved wine glasses. His sons were strictly educated in preparation for joining the family firm. They were sent to meet wine growers and shippers in

Bordeaux, Jerez, Epernay (for champagne) and Germany, where they learned everything about wine production and trade. They enlarged the customer list and obtained valuable contracts to supply army and navy messes, gentlemen's clubs and universities. In 1860, Harvey's business doubled when Prime Minister William Gladstone lowered the tax on French wine. By now Bristol had a growing affluent middle-class who wanted quality table wines, brandy, sherry, port and, of course, champagne. The smart new terraces and villas being built in Redland and Clifton had their own wine cellars waiting to be filled, and Harvey & Sons were on hand to give advice on stocking them and to take orders. John Harvey and his sons decided this was a good time to produce a new, smoother but less sweet version of their best-selling Bristol Milk. It was called Bristol Cream because, the story goes, a lady customer who was asked to compare Bristol Milk with the new blend announced: 'If that is Milk, then this is Cream.' Harvey's Bristol Cream became a world-famous brand, with sales going from strength to strength. Originally matured in bottles which gave it a concentrated flavour, it is a unique blend of several wines which together give it its distinctive smooth, creamy character.

When John Harvey died, in 1879, his obituary read: 'A more upright kinder man could not be – one who recognising his duty as a citizen in all its bearing, did it promptly and generously and unostentatiously.' Two of his sons continued to navigate the firm skilfully and successfully through both good and tough times. They picked up a royal warrant and expanded into new world markets. The next generation of sons (daughters and wives never inherited the business) saw the firm survive the Great War in Europe, prohibition in the USA, and then the Depression. They also had to embrace new ideas in marketing and advertising and adapt to modern processes, methods of supply and new fashions. The clientele was changing too; the age of gentlemen's clubs, private cellars and the laying down of port for the birth of a son were fading out. Sherry parties, meanwhile, became all the rage, and increasingly customers wanted to buy wine by the bottle at off-licences or grocers. Several succeeding generations of Harveys continued to run the company until it was taken over by Allied Domecq. But the name of Harvey's (and its age-old rival Averys) is still a vital part of the Bristol scene.

PACKAGING

Until surprisingly recently, the housewife went shopping with a calico or string bag and her grocer sold food loose and wrapped it in a piece of paper 'twiddled' up at the end. Butter was scooped out of barrels, cheese portions cut with wire, flour, sugar, sweets and biscuits were weighed and put in paper bags; bacon and sausages were cut to order and wrapped in oiled paper or old newspaper. Apart from some bottled products, such as Hotwells water and the imported wines and sherry blends which had made Bristol's bottle-making industry famous, almost nothing came pre-packaged as it does today. But yet another pioneering Bristol family dynasty was to change all that.

Elisha Smith Robinson, the son of a Gloucestershire papermaker, set up his own business in Bristol in 1844 making wrapping paper and handmade paper bags for food shops. By 1860, Robinson had grand premises at No 2 Redcliffe Street, selling 'plain and coloured tea-papers, reams of brown wrapping-paper and great quantities of hand-made paper bags'. Using the latest machinery and printing techniques, Robinson's mass-produced cartons, bags and sacks for numerous products, including Jones' self-raising flour and Fry's chocolates. Moving with the times, they used ornamental lettering and elaborate shading to print advertisements for the food suppliers on their bags and embraced new materials such as cellophane and waxed paper, especially useful for wrapping sticky sweets, raw meat and bread.

Numerous pioneering Bristol businesses such as the Frys, Joneses and Robinsons made important contributions to the new foods that revolutionised eating in the late nineteenth century. It became the age of the grocer, with his pre-packed teas, dried soups, tins of sweetened condensed milk, tinned meats and vegetables, ready-shredded suet, bottled chutneys, custard powder, processed bread and cheeses, and an increasingly cheap range of packeted, bottled and tinned foods displayed on the shelves.

BUILDING A MODERN PORT

The success of new food developments, and of pioneering food families, was highly dependent on efficient transport links. Bristol's trade in food and drink had always been a central ingredient in its success as a commercial port, but the voyage up the heavily tidal Avon, which had once made the port so secure during its earliest years, had long been a liability. Swift tides, fog and the steep mud banks were dangerous and difficult for the increasingly large vessels attempting to navigate their way up the seven miles of treacherous river to Bristol's City Dock. Heavily laden ships often became stranded on mud; some broke their backs and blocked the river to other traffic for several months. Over the centuries, the city authorities had made various ambitious and expensive attempts to solve the problem. In the Middle Ages, the course of the river Frome was changed and the 'Great Ditch' constructed. In 1712, Joshua Franklyn, a Bristol merchant, hoping to avoid the river altogether, attempted to bring the docks nearer to the sea. He sank a fortune in building a tide-free dock on the site of the old Roman *Portus Abona*. But, with no proper transport to take the goods back to Bristol, the dock was a commercial failure. It was

Brunel and the 'Clifton Puff'

Railways were the major means of quickly and cheaply transporting merchandise and were therefore a particular attraction for Bristol. Numerous companies and schemes were dreamed up, then dropped, and then revived. Isambard Kingdom Brunel proposed the construction of the Great Western Railway from Bristol to London. It finally opened in 1841 and Brunel's soaring viaducts, vast tunnels, impressive stations and Italianate bridges made him Bristol's greatest engineering hero.

Brunel's most impressive achievement was the Bristol suspension bridge. His designs were accepted in 1831 but delayed by the Bristol riots of that year and other problems meant that, sadly, the bridge was not finished until after his death. When finally completed, in 1864, the public turned out in huge numbers for the opening ceremony, which was carried off with great fanfare, drinking, feasting and rejoicing. Specially created for the occasion was the 'Clifton Puff', described as 'a traditional small cake which is rich yet light'.

The filling:

8oz peeled cored and chopped apples

8oz currants

4oz seedless raisins

1 cup candied peel, chopped

2 cups blanched almonds, chopped

half teaspoon grated nutmeg

4-6 tablespoons brandy

To be encased in puff pastry.

Mix ingredients well and leave in warm place for 1 hour. Roll out pastry thinly and cut into 4-inch squares. Put mixture on half of square and fold over making triangles. Brush with beaten egg, dust with sugar and bake at 400°F for 15-20 minutes.

instead used by privateers to repair and refit their ships out of sight of the authorities, and later a whaling company brought whales there and boiled their blubber. But the idea of a tide-free dock was a good one and engineers later took it back into the city, where a 'floating harbour' was dug out, with locks to keep the Frome permanently full. With little more than buckets and spades, the navvies also excavated a New Cut to take the tidal flow of the Avon. Inevitably the project took longer than planned and went way over budget, but when it was finished ships could enter the harbour, designed by London

Wreck of the Demerara, Samuel Loxton. Courtesy Bristol City Reference Library

engineer William Jessop, to load and unload without becoming stranded on mud on the ebb tide.

To celebrate the opening of the floating harbour 1,000 of the labourers who had 'sweated their labour' on the project were entertained to a 'bumper dinner'. The bill of fare consisted of 'two oxen, roasted whole, a proportionate weight of potatoes, and six hundredweight of plum pudding and a gallon of strong beer for each guest'. The inevitable result was fighting between English and Irish navvies. The Irishmen, according to a local reporter, 'attempted to take possession of a cart bringing up fresh supplies of "stingo" [slang for strong beer] and when they failed in their attempt, ran off in a rage to arm themselves with "shillelaghs" [cudgels]'. The hostile camps met in Prince's Street for a 'battle royal'. The authorities called in the press gang, which seized several of the 'drunken malefactors' for their own purposes.

But the new floating harbour could not solve the problem of increasingly large ships needing to use the river. The Industrial Revolution had caused a great change in shipbuilding, with steam power bringing about a very rapid increase in tonnage. Huge vessels continued to be constructed in Bristol, from where, in 1838, Brunel launched his mighty *Great Western* and later the *Great Britain* – neither could easily return to their berth and instead docked in the

LAUNCH OF THE GREAT BRITAIN STEAM SHIP.

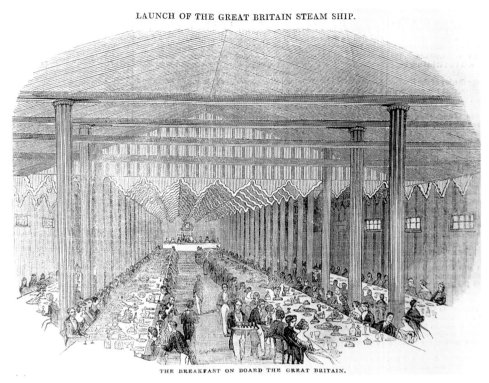

THE BREAKFAST ON BOARD THE GREAT BRITAIN.

The banquet on board ss *Great Britain* to celebrate its launch in 1843, from the *Illustrated London News*

Mersey. Things came to a head in November 1851, when the newly launched 3,000-ton paddle steamer, *Demerara*, was being towed downriver. She broke from her moorings, the tide swung her across the river and she was stuck in the mud. Thousands of people turned out to watch an army of workmen battle unsuccessfully to free the vessel. The second largest steamship afloat at that time, the *Demerara* had to be written off as a total wreck. This disaster struck a serious blow to Bristol's reputation as a port.

By the middle of the nineteenth century Britain had a thriving Empire, the Industrial Revolution was at full throttle and the railway system was expanding rapidly, but Bristol's port status was sliding into decline. Shortsighted administration, very high harbour dues charged in Bristol as compared to rival ports (Bristol's rates for unloading sugar and tobacco were nearly double those in Liverpool), overcharging of dock tolls and inefficient running of the docks, plus the shrinking of traditional West-Country industries such as woollen cloth, all contributed further to the problem. Once ranked the second city in England, Bristol was now relegated to a position behind the expanding manufacturing and trading cities of the north. If it was going to regain ground, something drastic would have to be done. Various ambitious schemes were put forward, fought over and rejected. Finally it was agreed to construct an entirely new port at the mouth of the Avon; thus avoiding the river altogether. In 1877, the new, privately funded Avonmouth Dock was at last ready for business. Once again, in true Bristol fashion, celebrations were in order, and after processions to the dock for the opening ceremony, the local people sat down to a hearty luncheon of '8 cwts prime beef, 200 quarters bread, and 3 cwts plum pudding'. Three bands played music whilst 500 children were later given tea at which '20 lbs tea, 10 gallons milk, 60 lbs sugar, 35 lbs butter, 2 cwts excellent cake and 100 quarters bread' were consumed.

Then, in 1879, another private venture, south of the rivermouth at Portishead, opened a rival commercial and passenger dock. Suddenly the Bristol City Dock Company found itself in competition with two huge and vastly superior complexes on its doorstep. In 1884, Bristol Corporation somehow raised sufficient funds to purchase both Avonmouth and Portishead docks and the three docks were combined to become the Port of Bristol Authority. Avonmouth Dock was still too small for the largest modern ships and so a vast new complex was built there capable of accommodating ocean-going liners. Known as the Royal Edward Dock, it was opened in 1908 by King Edward VII and Queen Alexandra. Bristol had finally become a modern seaport.

GOING BANANAS

There is one important tale of the docks which takes Bristol into the twentieth century and introduces an exotic new food. A month after the funeral of Queen Victoria, on 19 March 1901, the Bristol press reported the arrival of the first banana boat in Avonmouth Dock – the first, in fact, to arrive on British shores – to a tumultuous welcome. The ss *Port Morant* carried 20,000 bunches of bananas 'in excellent condition' and 14,000 boxes of oranges. When dockers unloaded the first cargo of bananas from Jamaica they were still almost unknown in England, and the headmaster of Avonmouth School considered the arrival to be such an historic event that he took his pupils down to the dock to join the crowd. A cartload of bananas was later sent round to the school for the children. But they had no idea how the strange new fruit should be eaten – unpeeled like apples or skins removed like oranges? One boy, who later recalled the day bananas first came to the school, said he ate so many they made him sick.

Almost overnight, the exotic banana became an everyday food. It also re-established Bristol's links with Jamaica and the Caribbean. The abolition of slavery in 1833 had meant that the sugar-growing plantations in the West Indies could not compete economically with sugar beet grown in Europe. Plantation owners had tried other crops, including cocoa and coffee, but the

Elders & Fyffes' banana boat/passenger liner *Ariguani* at Avonmouth, a popular visitor to the city.
photograph courtesy Colin Momber

banana, which the Portuguese were then growing in the Canary Islands, showed most promise. In 1900, the Colonial Secretary Joseph Chamberlain, anxious to help Britain's colony of Jamaica, set up a new postal and passenger service to the island, and to help cover costs, the shipping line of Elders & Fyffes, based in Avonmouth, would carry Caribbean bananas, pineapples and citrus fruits on the return voyage. Banana boats began to arrive regularly at Avonmouth, weekly in summer and fortnightly in winter. In order for the bananas to arrive in perfect condition, the fruit was picked in a green, unripe state and slowly ripened on the long journey. Each stem of fruit had to be unloaded singly, one man per stem, and carried from the ship to the strawed and steam-heated railway vans waiting alongside. This required hundreds of labourers, who called the purpose-built steamships, with their distinctive yellow funnels, 'Plum Boats', because it was a 'plum of a job' with three days guaranteed work and good pay.

By 1900, Bristol was criss-crossed with trams and omnibuses and surrounded by a network of busy canals, railways and well-made roads, making it possible for traders to speedily transport their goods, especially fresh foods, to markets anywhere around the country. John Hodgson was a market trader whose business would take full advantage of transportation links. The son of the landlord of the Pilgrim Inn near Bristol Bridge, he grew up surrounded by the colourful sights and sounds of nearby St Nicholas Market – with its stalls of butter, cheese, eggs, poultry and bacon and market gardeners selling their fresh produce. He loved the lively atmosphere of market life and he also fell in love with Emma, a young girl who came every week from the Mendips to sell rabbits – a popular cheap meat at the time. In 1895, John and Emma were married and set up their own stall selling fruit and vegetables. By 1910 the couple were operating six market stalls and retail shops in Redcliffe Hill and Stapleton Road. They bought 150 acres of land at Frenchay, where they established a market garden producing fresh vegetables and soft fruits to supply their shops and stalls. More importantly, they also constructed specially designed buildings for ripening the green bananas coming off the Fyffes banana boats at Avonmouth. It was the first of its kind in the country and very soon the processing and distribution of bananas became their main business, with Hodgson lorries loaded with bananas a familiar sight.

WARTIME BRISTOL 1900-1945

YOU ARE WHAT YOU EAT

When recruits for the Boer War turned up at Bristol's Horfield Barracks in 1899, the authorities were appalled to discover how many of them were unfit to fight. Thirty eight per cent of volunteers were malnourished, undersized and debilitated by years of inadequate diet. This shocking revelation woke the Government from a blind disregard for the health of its poorer citizens and led social investigators to ask: if so many men needed to fight were unfit, what about their families?

'It is no exaggeration to say that the opening of the twentieth century saw malnutrition more rife in England than it had been since the dearths of medieval and Tudor times', Professor Jack Drummond later wrote in his book *The Englishman's Food* (1939). Few middle-class people were even aware of the terrible distress suffered in poor urban districts until R. Seebohm Rowntree, son of the Quaker social reformer and member of the great chocolate-manu-facturing dynasty, published a report on poverty in 1901. He revealed that the average working-class family in cities such as York, London and Bristol was struggling to pay for rent, clothing and food and lived on the borders of star-vation, on a diet of potatoes, rice, cheap sausages or faggots, tea and bread and dripping or suet pudding. Generations of children were stunted, anaemic, toothless and suffering from skin diseases, rickets, tuberculosis, beriberi and other diet-related disabilities.

Theories linking health with diet go back a very long way; the Greeks and Romans preached some extraordinary ideas about bodily 'humours', claiming that certain foods were beneficial and others harmful. This was mostly nonsense, scientifically, but it persisted for many centuries. However, country people had long ago learned, through trial and error, which plants picked from the hedgerows were good for health and which helped treat various complaints, and this knowledge was passed on through the generations. But

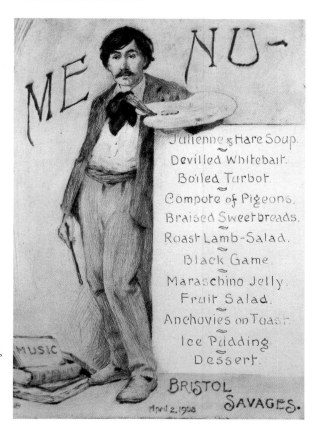

ME NU -

Julienne & Hare Soup.
~
Devilled Whitebait.
~
Boiled Turbot.
~
Compote of Pigeons.
~
Braised Sweetbreads.
~
Roast Lamb-Salad.
~
Black Game.
~
Maraschino Jelly.
Fruit Salad.
~
Anchovies on Toast.
~
Ice Pudding.
~
Dessert.

BRISTOL
SAVAGES.

April 2. 1908

A lavish menu from the 'Edwardian summer' of pre-war days: the artists' group Bristol Savages, April 1908. Etching by Stanley Anderson

it was not until well into the twentieth century that scientists really understood about nutrition and vitamins. Scurvy, the sailors' scourge, had been connected to a lack of fresh fruit and vegetables during the Napoleonic Wars, but vitamin C was not identified as the real factor until 1912.

As researchers soon concluded, it wasn't just soldiers whose health affected the nation; if the workers were malnourished, industry suffered too. When Rowntree argued that poverty was the result of low wages, it went against the traditionally held view that the poor were responsible for their own plight. In January 1908, a meeting was held by the Bristol Socialist Society to consider the unemployment situation in the city. Ernest Bevin, then a young truck driver delivering bottled lemonade around Bristol, and a member of the Society, addressed the meeting. Five hundred bags of food and cups of coffee were handed to the hungry men who attended. The meeting passed a resolution condemning the inaction of the Government in alleviating the conditions of the poor. A month later, General Booth of the Salvation Army visited Bristol and addressed a meeting at the Victoria Rooms. Unrest, strikes and union activities in Bristol grew more numerous and vocal. Some factories, such as

J.S. Fry's and W.D. & H.O. Wills', distributed surplus food from the workers' canteens to the poor. In March that year the Bristol Education Committee resolved to provide school dinners for 1,300 children. Meals were cooked from a central kitchen with local produce and sent out in vehicles supplied by local tradespeople. In 1916, a committee of scientists set up by the Royal Society in London made the startlingly obvious discovery that 'a slight reduction of food below the necessary amount … meant lower output and fewer profits'. Perhaps low wages were counterproductive after all.

In the early 1900s, aged 14, Helen Rider started life as a kitchen maid in Westbury-on-Trym, earning 2s 6d a week and working from 6 am until 10 or 11 pm at night. 'My employers were shooting and fishing people, often they'd come back late at night and hand me birds to pluck or rabbits to skin and I'd be up until midnight.' But she at least had board and lodgings, security and plenty to eat. Her family lived in a cottage near Long Ashton, 'eight in a two bedroomed house with a privy at the end of the garden and a well four doors away'. 'They was hard times alright', she wrote. Another woman, from Bedminster, recalled that her meagre wages were all that came into her family home. 'We didn't starve,' she wrote, 'but it was a very thin diet of bread and potatoes. Our treat was to take turns to dip bread into a bowl of one egg beaten up with water.' 'It was always bread with something', another woman recalled; 'jam on bread, dripping on bread, sauce on bread, cod liver oil and malt on bread'.

The years between the death of Queen Victoria and the outbreak of the Great War are often referred to as the 'Edwardian Summer' – despite the fact it was not especially sunny, either literally or, for many, metaphorically. The Edwardian era was actually a period of appalling inequality. Whilst philanthropists worried about the poor, political activists roused the workers and scientists struggled to understand nutrition, the rich upper classes blithely continued to have a thoroughly good time. Encouraged by their self-indulgent king, Edward VII, known as 'Tum Tum', the affluent built themselves luxurious modern houses for entertaining equipped with bathrooms and electricity and surrounded by large gardens with tennis courts and swimming pools. Guests were invited to such places by telephone and travelled speedily by railway and car to meet up for lavish weekend house parties. One tends to think of Edwardian house parties taking place in grand country estates, but there were several large houses in and around Bristol where the wealthy 'new rich' entertained on a scale far more ambitious and grandiose than Ellen Sharples could have dreamed of. Respectable families such as the Wills tobacco barons, the Frys chocolate pioneers and the sherry-importing Harveys owned substantial countrified houses in the Leigh Woods area; the Gibbs families at

The fruit and flower market in High Street, the fish market in Nicholas Street. 1906, and Easter Monday on Durdham Down. Drawings by Samuel Loxton. Courtesy Bristol Reference Library

Tyntesfield and Barrow Court, who made their fortune importing guano from Peru for fertiliser, did not quite fit the hedonistic image of Edwardian high life, but they certainly knew how to entertain.

Wealthy Edwardians had a mania for the open air and exercise; tennis, cricket, boating, bicycling, shooting and fishing parties and horseriding gave them hearty appetites for large, lavish meals. Before the Great War took them there were armies of servants who rose at dawn to ensure the Edwardian breakfast table was groaning with a delicious spread and offered a huge choice of tempting dishes such as poached eggs and bacon, devilled kidneys, kedgeree, cold game, finnan haddock, sliced tongue and potted shrimps, as well as numerous kinds of breads, fancy buns and pastries spread with whisky-flavoured marmalade, plus fruit from the hothouse – all washed down with freshly brewed Indian or China tea, coffee or chocolate. Later, the gentlemen would drift into the smoking room, leaving the ladies who had not ordered breakfast in bed to idle over their tea and wonder what to do with the day. Luncheon was often an open-air picnic during breaks from shooting or fishing. Hampers, brought out by footmen, were filled with tempting rich game pies, cold meats and warming soups. For those who preferred to stay in the house there was afternoon tea to look forward to, with thinly sliced bread and butter, cucumber or egg sandwiches and tea cakes or scones with thick yellow cream and homemade jams. In the evening, several hours were spent changing for dinner and meeting for cocktails and champagne before everyone sat down to a five-course meal. Edwardian fine dining was richly tasty and exquisitely presented but it had none of the colourful extravagance and culinary drama of Roman or Norman cuisines.

'BRAVO BRISTOL!'

At the outbreak of the Great War, the health of ordinary workers hardly seemed to have changed and a man's height was still an issue for recruiting officers. There were so many men of below average height that the Bristol Recruiting Committee received War Office approval to form an infantry battalion for recruits whose height was between 5' and 5' 3"; it became known as the West of England Bantams. But this was not the sort of army Lord Kitchener, the Secretary of State for War, was planning. In August 1914, he sent a telegram to the Bristol Citizens Recruiting Committee sanctioning the formation of a battalion of 'better class young men'. An appeal was sent out to clubs, banks, insurance and merchants' offices, manufacturers, brokers and large retailers for 'Athletic, Mercantile and Professional young men'. In less than a month, the 'Bristol's Own' battalion was full strength with enthusiastic,

Bristol soldiers march past a tram advertising Fry's cocoa c.1914, Fry's supplied chocolate to British forces in huge quantities

well-fed young volunteers. Frederic E. Weatherly, a barrister and prolific song-writer from Portishead, wrote lyrics for a wartime recruitment song, 'Bravo Bristol', which was set to music by Ivor Novello. Weatherly also wrote lyrics for the famous songs 'Danny Boy' and 'Roses of Picardy'. Over 1,000 young volunteers went to the Front and 800 of the original Bristol's Own were killed, with hundreds more wounded.

By 1914, Britain's declining agricultural sector had left it heavily dependent on importing more than 60 per cent of the country's food supplies and 80 per cent of its wheat. Now German U-boats attacked ships carrying essential food. Food rationing was introduced and civilians at home were almost starved into submission. Soldiers on the front line, however, had dull but adequate rations of tinned food such as 'bully beef', dried vegetables, bread and packets of biscuits, cheese, jam, dried fruit and butter, plus generous allowances of rum, porter, chocolate and tobacco. Although they were trying to live on rapidly vanishing food supplies at home, mothers and wives sent their menfolk food parcels including Trench Cake, which kept well during the long period in the post, plus Fry's chocolate bars and packets of tea.

When men went off to the trenches, women took their places in the factories, shops and offices. After the war, employers found women cheaper to employ than men and some refused to take the returning troops back, which caused much bitterness. The chocolate and tobacco factories advertised specifically for girls; Fry's was a particularly popular employer because of its generous welfare facilities including sports, schools and free breakfasts. Employment with Fry's followed strict and religious rules. Workers each received a Bible and had to attend morning worship; women were expected to leave when they got married and were given a copy of Mrs Beeton's *Book of Household Management* to instruct them as mothers and housewives.

Despite the continuing poverty and economic slump in Britain between the two world wars, Bristol was relatively less badly off than other cities. The wide range of industry helped it to avoid the worst results of the economic depression of the thirties. Employment was high in the thriving new industries turning out aeroplanes, tobacco, paint, footwear and paper. Huge quantities of food such as wheat from America and frozen meat from Australia and South America was imported through Bristol's docks, keeping dock workers and merchant sailors in constant employment. Though there were lean periods and the unemployed did suffer, those who were employed weren't short of a bob or two to spend on their pleasure and some nicer food with a bit more choice. They could enjoy free sports facilities, coach trips, outings to the zoo or a day on steamers up the Bristol Channel; an evening tram ride into town to window-shop or a visit to the theatre, such as the Prince's, the Empire, the Hippodrome or the Theatre Royal; a concert at the Colston Hall or a film at one of the numerous new cinemas opening up, followed by drinks at the pub and even, as a special treat, a 'dinner and dance' at a hotel. Bristol suburbs based on the new garden suburbs in London were exploding outwards, gradually replacing the city's slums. Fry's huge factory moved out of the congested city to a new site at Somerdale, Keynsham.

The author and playwright, J.B. Priestley, travelled through England in the autumn of 1933. When he came to Bristol, a city he particularly loved, he wrote:

It is a genuine city, an ancient metropolis … The Merchant Venturers have vanished; the slave trade, on whose evil proceeds this city flourished once, is now only a reminder of man's cruelty to man; the port, depending on the shallow twisting Avon, is only a shadow of its old self; but Bristol lives on, indeed arrives at a new prosperity, by selling us Gold Flake and Fry's chocolate and soap and clothes and a hundred other things. And the smoke from a million gold flakes solidifies into a new Gothic Tower for the university and the chocolate melts away only to leave behind it all the fine big shops down Park Street, the pleasant villas out at Clifton, and an occasional glass of Harvey's Bristol Milk for nearly everybody.

Priestley described a great city with beautiful old buildings, a thriving university, a port with ships and pubs, and ancient streets lined with shops crowded with 'working people who enjoy life'. It was a fine portrait of a city that was soon to change almost out of recognition.

MAKING DO IN THE KITCHEN, 1939-1945

When the Williams family sat down for their Christmas dinner in 1940, in their newly built suburban house in Knowle, they were already familiar with the wartime concepts of 'making do' and 'going without'. For most people turkey was unaffordable and a family of four's weekly meat ration wouldn't even cover the cost of a small chicken. Mr and Mrs Williams and their three children, plus Grandma, were fortunate to have a piece of pork belly sent 'from Uncle A's farm on the Levels', with plenty of potatoes, swedes and carrots roasted in the dripping and some boiled greens. During the autumn, Mrs Williams had made a Christmas pudding; mixing a bit of suet and flour with some dried plums and hazelnuts which the children had gathered on trips to the countryside. Custard was made with dried eggs and milk and 'a drop of vanilla I found at the back of the cupboard leftover from better days', she told a reporter on the Bristol *Evening World*. There were no crackers to pull or silly hats to be worn or bad jokes to shout out. But decorations were made with strips of painted newspaper glued together and the tree was cut from the top of an old pine 'that was too big for its boots anyway ... we later burned it in the fireplace, so no waste there'. Although Christmas was a muted affair, there was still panto with Red Riding Hood at the Theatre Royal, variety at the Hippodrome, Gary Cooper starring in *The Westerner* at the cinema and free carol singing in Bristol Cathedral.

Bristol's worst suffering had begun in November 1940, with terrible bombing raids which carried on until the following summer. Over 2,000 civilians were killed or seriously injured and many thousands of homes were destroyed and people made homeless. The 'City of Churches' became a city of ruins, with many of its ancient buildings lost. On 17 December, *The Western Daily Press* reported the king's visit to Bristol to see the bomb damage. Crowds of factory girls, working men, housewives and children lined the streets waving Union Jacks and shouting bravely 'we can take it'. 'I know you will' replied His Majesty as he toured the city's ruins, including the Jacobean St Peter's Hospital, the Norman churches of St Peter's, St Nicholas and St Mary le Port and the seventeenth-century timber-framed Dutch House.

Less than a third of the food in Britain at the start of World War II was produced at home, and, mirroring World War I, the enemy quickly targeted incoming ships with their vital supplies of fruit, sugar, cereals and refrigerated meat. Loading and unloading the precious cargo of armaments and food from merchant vessels at Bristol's Avonmouth docks was a particularly dangerous job; the longer a ship was docked, the more vulnerable it became to German bombers. Ships came in on one tide, were quickly unloaded, and sailed out on the next. If several ships followed one another on subsequent tides, men often did not return home for two or three days and nights. Dockworkers even worked through air raids while a lookout on deck watched for enemy planes; when he shouted 'Down', the men fell to the deck and waited for the next command: 'Carry on lads'. The Bristol press reported daily acts of courage during attacks on the city. The chef of the bombed-out restaurant at Jones' Department Store in St Mary le Port Street took his pots and pans onto the pavement, donned his chef's hat and prepared lunch in the open air. Mrs Bamberger, 'that gallant woman', drove her mobile canteen to the worst spots every night to serve tea and sandwiches to rescue squads. One newspaper carried the headline 'Proud to be a citizen of Blitzol!'

The battle on the kitchen front began with the declaration of war in September 1939. The Government, keen to learn from its mistakes in the Great War when food stocks were seriously depleted, quickly set up a Ministry of Food, headed by Lord Woolton. By January 1940, food rationing was part of everyone's daily lives. Every individual had a ration book and personal food allowance depending on their age and circumstance. Children, pregnant women and the sick had extra milk, orange juice and cod liver oil and people doing heavy work were permitted more. One person's typical weekly allowance would be: one fresh egg; 4 oz margarine and bacon (about four rashers); 2 oz butter and tea; 1 oz cheese; and 8 oz sugar. Meat was allowed by price, so cheaper cuts were popular. Points could be pooled or saved to buy pulses, cereals, tinned goods, dried fruit, biscuits and jam. The worst thing was the queuing for hours at a shop only to find – when you finally got to the front – that what you wanted had gone. News of any source of food went round like wildfire and you had to be quick to take advantage. A woman from Redland heard that fat was available at a tripe factory and set off at dawn to walk several miles for the 'treat'. But the fat was so disgusting, she never tried it again.

With so few basic ingredients such as fats, eggs, onions or sugar available, it was a constant struggle to find ways to give the family nutritious and appetising meals: 'I remember the sweet my mother used to make out of dried milk and scrambled eggs made with powdered egg.' Alternative pastry recipes included this one:

To make a pastry without fat:
Mix together 8 oz wheat meal flour, 1 teaspoon baking powder, pinch

salt and pinch powdered sage. Stir in nearly ¼ pint of cold milk or milk and water. Roll out the mixture and use it as you would an ordinary crust.

One young Bristol girl described how a relative visited and helped himself to a hunk of homemade bread and a big lump of cheese: 'I remember my mother's distress that he had just eaten four people's ration of cheese for the week.' Every housewife was galvanised into patriotism and thrift to make something out of very little. Meals had to be ingenious, cheap and nutritious – quite a challenge on wartime rations; small amounts of meat with chopped potatoes and carrots made good pasties; stews could be filled out with pulses or dumplings. For the average housewife racking her brains to produce meals, having to cope with factory work, childcare and housekeeping, the need to master the maths of ever-changing and complex ration rules was a huge added strain. Her life was crammed with unceasing information and instruction, finger wagging and advice on what to do and what not to do with food, and how not to waste it. The Ministry of Food produced posters and leaflets which were distributed and published in all the newspapers: 'Waste the Food and Help the Hun!' and 'A sailor's blood is on your head if you waste a scrap of bread!' – a particularly poignant and cruel slogan for Bristolians. Informative 'Food Flashes' were shown in cinemas and BBC Radio transmitted the daily five-minute 'Kitchen Front', bombarding listeners with rules, regulations and 'good ideas', featuring numerous recipes based on carrots, potatoes and dried eggs. There was even a leaflet with instructions for what was called 'interrupted cooking', when the housewife was 'called away for an air raid in the middle of preparing a meal'. (The most important thing, of course, was to remember to turn off the gas cooker.) Advice for keeping food moist and warm included placing it between two plates and leaving the stewpot in the turned-off oven, 'where it will continue to cook nicely whilst you are away'. Some things, however, apparently never survived an air raid: 'Let's face it,' wrote one Bristol housewife, 'fish and chips don't face up well to air raids.' Mrs Mary Coleman of Coldharbour Road remembered:

I had just put some bacon in the pan when the sirens went. My husband was sitting waiting for his tea, already in his warden's uniform. As the first barrage started the bacon was beginning to sizzle. I turned the gas off and my husband grabbed his tin hat and respirator and said: 'that sounds like us'. I wished him 'Cheerio' and got our hide-out under the stairs ready for the children. Pillows, blankets and a hot-water bottle filled with warm milk and a tin of biscuits for the babies and some cigarettes for me.

The chef from Jones's department store sets up an impromptu kitchen for firefighters and rescuers in the bombed-out ruins. Courtesy Bristol Record Office

This recipe for 'All Clear' Sandwiches might have come in handy:

> Spread fish or meat paste on to bread and margarine. Wash young dandelion leaves and spread on top and cover with a second slice of bread and margarine.

Everyone tried to do their bit and cut down on something. The traditional big dinners that Bristol merchants and officials so loved had to go, although the Bristol Savages – a group of artists based at the Red Lodge – continued their charity-raising feasts by calling them 'nosebag luncheons'. Each member brought their own food, though drink was still supplied. Vegetarians were allowed to exchange meat rations for extra cheese and eggs. One extraordinary book, *Eat Well in Wartime*, advocated a vegetarian diet by pointing out that 'it can be both pleasant and healthy because Hitler and Mussolini – and our George Bernard Shaw – are vegetarian and whatever else one may think of them they are all men of strength and energy'.

The National Loaf was launched in 1942. Made with nourishing whole-meal, it was dry and grey and quickly nicknamed 'Hitler's secret weapon'. With barely any butter, jam, even margarine or dripping, to spread on it, the bread was universally loathed. Woolton Pie, named after the Minister of Food, was the last straw. The Bristol Food Control Committee in Whiteladies Road published regular directives to shops and food producers. Offal was off-rations and butchers were told to encourage women to cook dishes made with liver, heart, tripe and brains. Cake making was particularly difficult; dried eggs made them crumble and icing sugar was forbidden. Carrots were used to sweeten cakes and wedding cakes were often decorated with painted cardboard. Ingenious substitutes were made for a whole variety of usually ordinary foods like onions, eggs, cheese, tomatoes, sausages, meat, fish, cakes, biscuits, chocolate, apples, oranges and lemons. The war introduced a crop of unique recipes that modern cooks would admire for their cunning and imagination but probably would not have enjoyed eating.

Home-front housewives were urged to be creative with 'mock' recipes which included 'cream' made with margarine, milk and cornflour. Powdered egg and tinned sweetened milk were store-cupboard mainstays while Oxo, Bisto and Marmite were essential standbys for flavouring sauces, soups and stews. The Americans sent strange cans of economy meat such as Spam (Supply Pressed American Meat), Prem, corned beef, Tang and Mor. Some food was beyond eating: eggs pickled in isinglass (fishes' swim bladders) and odd 'new' fish such as saith and ling, whalemeat and the disgusting tinned snoek. There was even that old Bristol staple, salt cod, which had to be boiled until it resembled 'flannelette'. Family pets, if not too fussy, rarely went hungry when these foods were on offer.

> When fisherfolk are brave enough
> To face the mines and foe for you
> You surely can be brave enough
> To face a fish that's new.

With shortages in World War I still a vivid memory, the country had to start growing more of its own food. The Government created the 'Dig for Victory' initiative and ordered that vast acres of unploughed land be cultivated, including Windsor Great Park, which became the largest wheat field in the country. By 1944, home food production had almost doubled. Households were expected to dig up their back gardens and grow whatever they could, even in towns. They were planted with greens, potatoes, beans and carrots. One resident of

WARTIME COOKING

Soups
These used shredded stalks of broccoli, turnip and beetroot tops, even bean-and pea pods, with lots of chopped parsley or mustard for flavouring and bulked up with oatmeal. Ham Bone Purée (rather like an old-fashioned pottage) was a popular standby, with split peas, haricot beans or lentils.

Fish
England's coastline was covered in barbed wire, mines and booby traps, and fishing was a dangerous business. Despite fishing along the west coast and up the Bristol Channel being less dangerous, there was little fresh fish to be had and fish dishes were mostly made with dried or tinned sardines, herring, salmon and the loathed snoek (a kind of barracuda which is quite pleasant eaten fresh but horrible from a tin). Sardine pancakes with tomato sauce and salmon in custard were agreeable, while Fish and Leek Pudding, with a suet paste, was said to be a favourite of Neville Chamberlain, then prime minister.

Meat
For a meat-eating nation, meat rationing was a national bad joke. It is said that women invariably went without in order to provide enough meat for their men and children. Even then, it was usually a poor substitute: stuffed ear, pig's feet in jelly, Mock Goose, Hash of Calves Head, Melt and Skirt Pudding and Lights (which, Ambrose Heath wrote, his cat would not touch). Horse meat, venison from rustled deer and poached rabbit and wood pigeon – even city birds – were offered at the butchers 'under the counter'. Sausages had little meat and were mostly made with bread along with some chopped cow's udders, melts and other 'unmentionable' bits. Roast chicken was a forgotten luxury – hens were kept for precious eggs and only eaten when their laying days were over. There were numerous recipes for common birds such as Somerset Rook Pie with Figgy Paste, made with currants and raisins; Crow à la Lyonnaise, garnished with fried onions and vinegar; 'Sparrow (or lark) Pie'; or thrushes wrapped in bacon and fried with tomatoes.

DIG for victory NOW!

Vegetables

Potatoes became king. They were full of vitamin C, easy to grow and simple to cook, either boiled, mashed, baked or stuffed. Potatoes were used as a substitute in pastry, scones and cakes, to make flan cases and pie coverings, grated instead of suet and mixed to bulk out meat and fish soups and stews. Carrots and cabbage came a close second with parsnip not far behind. Carrot and parsnip were especially popular as sweeteners. Carrots replaced sugar in cakes and biscuits; children even ate them raw instead of sweets. There were ingenious vegetable recipes for Baked Vegetable Roll with a potato pastry and Mushroom Puffs. Beat the Cold used warming red beetroot and some grated horseradish while Marrow Surprise made watery, tasteless marrow less dull with a topping of toasted cheese.

Woolton Pie

The pie was invented by the head chef at the Savoy and named after Lord Woolton, the Minister of Food. The recipe involved dicing up and then cooking potatoes, parsnips, cauliflower, swede, carrots, turnip or other available vegetables. Rolled oats were added to thicken the vegetable water plus chopped spring onions, parsley and a teaspoon of vegetable extract for flavour. The dish was topped with potato pastry and possibly grated cheese, baked in a moderate oven until the pastry was nicely browned and served hot with a brown gravy.

'Patriotic' Puddings

Britain's sweet tooth suffered badly during the war (though the actual teeth were much healthier). It was the cook's greatest challenge to continue to produce popular puddings, cakes, biscuits, jams and sweets with very little sugar, eggs or dried fruit. But somehow they managed to come up with versions such as: Wartime Trifle using stale tea buns, cooked fruit or apple sauce and custard or potato flour; Siege Cake made with dripping or lard, buttermilk and golden syrup; Eggless, Fatless Walnut Cake and Wartime Christmas Cake without Eggs. Mock marzipan could be made with haricot beans, ground rice, margarine, some sugar and almond essence. The scum from jam making was valuable for use in many kinds of fruit puddings.

Bristol children eating post-war bananas

St George had grown a 'goodly crop' of potatoes but was reluctant to dig them up. Then, one night, the Germans dropped a bomb on his garden, blasting away every last spud. The next morning a small crowd stood surveying the scene. An old man was heard to say: 'Serves the old bugger right, I told 'im to dig un up only yesterday night.'

Rabbits and chickens were kept for meat and eggs and some even kept a pig in the backyard, which was fed on household waste and killed in the autumn, when fresh meat and preserves were prepared in the old traditional styles. Pig Clubs were started all over the country and parties went out to gather 'hedgerow harvests' of mushrooms, blackberries and wild fruits and nuts. People were relearning age-old ways of food production and preserving. Meat and fish leftovers were potted up and kept well, the old airtight pies and pasties became popular again, and there was extra sugar and vinegar allowance for people to make jams and chutneys from gluts of fruit and vegetables. Grandma's preserving pan was brought out and her own recipes for pickled meat and fish, salted beans, dried apple rings and marrow and beet chutney were carefully studied. 'We grew all our own vegetables and the children went into the surrounding countryside to gather blackberries, mushrooms and collect nuts and greenstuff', recalled one Bristolian family. 'We helped with harvest so we could glean for corn to feed our chickens and rabbits – it was like the old days, like being country folk again, but we had to learn how.' For many town dwellers it must have seemed they were going back to the days of their medieval ancestors when they had to be inventive with mock foods on fish days, get through the winter months and make do with whatever food was permitted or available.

The National Fruit and Cider Institute at Long Ashton (later called the Long Ashton Research Station) came up with all kinds of clever ideas to use up gluts of fruit, from powdered plums to apple treacle. They also created a concentrated blackcurrant juice loaded with vitamin C which was first distributed in hospitals and schools and later called Ribena. It was manufactured commercially by the Bristol drinks firm H.W. Carters & Co., which was soon producing thousand of bottles of the nation's favourite fruit drink.

Despite the stress of rationing and war, the health of the poor, and indeed everyone, improved; no one starved or was even malnourished. Thanks to Lord Woolton, people were encouraged to eat sufficient – but not too much – protein, carbohydrates, pulses and fruit and vegetables. The Government's humourless 'fighting diet' had produced an extraordinarily healthy nation. Statistics showed that the reduction of cholesterol led to a drop in heart and liver disease and the improved diet meant lower infant mortality, while plenty of milk and a near-sugarless diet led to a huge improvement in children's teeth as well as healthier bones and fewer cases of rickets.

After the war, Bristolians wanted to get their lives back to normal, forget about war and rationing and have something decent to eat. It wasn't enough to be told how healthy they had become on the wartime diet, they wanted to live a little, not just to exist. Yet for some time to come, life became even more austere, with the introduction of bread rationing in 1946 and sweet rations halved. Suddenly the docksides were piled high with tinned whalemeat and 10 million half-pound tins of snoek from South Africa. Whalemeat and snoek were the last straw – even the cat wouldn't touch them. Then bananas came back to Avonmouth and a new generation of schoolchildren ran down to the Avonmouth docks to be given armfuls of a fruit they had never seen or eaten.

FAST FOOD AND SLOW FOOD

EATING OUT

The restaurant as we know it today did not get properly established in English towns until Victorian times (and it was still a long way off that a respectable lady might be seen eating in a public dining room). Things began to look up around Bristol as a few smart restaurants opened for business – such as Hort's, which had a colourful history. It started life much earlier as a small coffee house in Wine Street run by a Mrs Greenway, whose daughter turned it into an inn and, in 1743, renamed it the Exchange Dining Rooms after the recently built Bristol Exchange, nearby on Corn Street. After she married William Hort, the city's rate collector, the inn became known as Hort's. It was one of the best places to eat in Bristol city centre, and its clientele included stockbrokers from the Exchange, merchants and lawyers, as well as gentlemen farmers who had come into the city to sell their livestock. Hort's signature dishes were oyster soup and Dover sole, and it is claimed that the first cocktails served in the city were mixed in Hort's bar – but only for men. The proprietors enforced a strict, no-women rule until the Great War, when wounded officers, returning home to convalesce in Bristol, complained there was nowhere they could take their wives. As a wartime concession, wives and nurses were allowed to sit discreetly in an upstairs room at Hort's.

Between the wars, more restaurants opened until there was plenty to choose from, including the Grand Hotel, St Stephen's Tavern, the Montague Arms and the Mauretania, with its decor of mahogany panelling and fittings bought from RMS *Mauretania* when she was scrapped in 1935. There were also numerous private clubs and societies where male members could drink and dine: Bristol Savages, Clifton Arts, Royal Empire Society, Bach Society, and the Speleological (caving) Society. The rest met in their favourite bars, such as the Sedan Chair, the ancient Llandoger Trow – with its old theatrical playbills and air of the Spanish Main – or the Rummer, which was still the venue of city merchants and civic dignitaries.

The popularity of street food and takeaway food in Bristol is built on a long tradition going back at least to the Middle Ages. Street vendors, selling goods from baskets and trays or from hand carts and small horse-drawn vans, were a common feature of Bristol life. Fresh milk from a cow kept in the city, a tray of homemade pies, fresh-picked flowers and all kinds of knick-knacks were carried round the street in search of passing customers or taken to the back doors of people's homes. Medieval cookshops once wafted their odours of roast meats and fresh-baked pies around streets and ships, attracting hungry townspeople and seamen. Centuries later, they could still buy similar kinds of pies, sausages, black puddings, saveloys, polonies and faggots with gravy and mash (made by local men such as Herbert Hill Brain of Upper York Street, who started selling faggots in the 1930s, and William Clark of Bedminster, who founded his pie business in 1909). It was all washed down with gallons of Bristol beer, brewed in the city's numerous small breweries. A journalist once asked a local customer at Clark's Pie Shop why he liked them so much. 'Clark's Pies is just Bristol, isn't it … I have come here for years. It's good old-fashioned grub and that's why I like it.'

In the early 1900s, supermarkets were still unheard of, fish and chips remained our undisputed national dish and the great British tradition of the ice-cream van was just around the corner. In 1925, Eugenio Verrecchia, whose family had emigrated from Italy, opened his first ice-cream parlour, the Modern Café, in Coronation Road. Several of his seven children expanded the business into more cafés and an ice-cream-making factory in Brislington and built up a fleet of vans which toured the city selling fresh-made ice-cream. They developed specially made vehicles, which, a local newspaper explained, meant 'in effect, that ice cream is made only minutes before it is served, unlike the days, and perhaps weeks, which the family brick type of ice remains in the refrigerator'. As these pioneering 'ice-cream machines on wheels' drove around the streets of Bristol ringing out their tune to queues of enthusiastic customers, they were able to make, freeze and serve dozens of varieties of delicious, fresh-made Italian ice-cream in cones filled by a tap similar to the miniature bar pump. Cones were a halfpenny or a penny and a dish of ice-cream with flavouring, twopence. The Verrecchia family were still selling gallons of their ice-cream up to the late 1990s and fighting off competition from giants such as Walls and Lyons. Whether it was faggots, pies or ice-cream, Bristolians continued to prefer the real thing: 'People want ice-cream as it used to be', claimed Betty Verrecchia; 'It's traditional home-made stuff … we Italians started it.'

Indeed, Italy and good, popular food seem to have been synonymous with eating out in Bristol. On Wednesday 17 June 1956, an entirely new kind of eating out was launched in the city – it was called the Berni Inn. Most people think of the Berni Inn as a very English or American idea but it was actually

Aldo Berni (left) with employee
Leo Connor

dreamed up by two Italians – Frank and Aldo Berni. The brothers had bought
and refurbished Bristol's historic Rummer Inn on All Saint's Lane by the old
St Nicholas Market, and transformed it into the first of what would became
a famous chain of restaurants where ordinary people could eat out cheaply. It
was the beginning of a revolution in British eating habits across the country.

Frank and Aldo were Welsh Italians whose family was among several who
had emigrated from Italy in Victorian times to run the network of Italian cafés
in the Welsh mining valleys. Known as *bracchi*, these cafés invariably served
soup, a joint and two vegetables to hungry miners and steelworkers. Frank
and Aldo opened some eating places of their own but in 1939, when war
broke out, Frank and another brother were interned as enemy aliens. Aldo,
however, had a British passport and carried on running the restaurants. At the
end of the war, the brothers moved to Bristol, where they bought Hort's
restaurant – by then in new premises in Broad Street. It was an impressive
place, with three floors of dining-rooms: the Chateaubriand grill, the oyster
bar and the chop and steak bar. Giant Dover soles or big, butch steaks were
the order of the day, and war-weary people could eat their fill. Then, in 1956,
the Aldo brothers heard that the Rummer Inn, near St Nicholas Market, was
up for sale. They snapped it up, gave it a total refurbishment and it became

June 1956: Bruna Golding welcomes her first customers to the Smuggler's Bar in the Rummer Berni Inn

the first Berni Inn.

When food rationing finally ended in 1954 and Bristol's citizens hankered after meat, the Berni brothers were determined to provide it. They served Argentinean steak, chips, peas and a roll and butter, plus pudding or cheese, at a fixed price of 7s 6d (37.5p). Along with plates piled high with good food were the famous 'schooners' of medium sherry, giving a huge boost to Bristol's traditional sherry business, which had been in decline during the war. A 'schooner' was a whole eighth of a bottle, served from a big barrel which stood behind the bar, and was considered very classy. Italian-born Bruna Golding worked at the Rummer Berni Inn from the start:

> It was the crème de la crème, all the bankers, businessmen and journalists came to eat there – but anyone could eat any time, any day; it was even open on Sunday. Bristol woke up and began eating out.

In the restaurant, the deep red-maroon velour plush banquettes, bare varnished tables and barrels of sherry behind the bar, coupled with the now-favourite menu of Prawn Cocktail, steak and Black Forest Gateau, added up to a huge success. The Berni Inn was a brilliant exercise in careful cost control and in knowing how to appeal to people sick of a dreary and meagre wartime diet and with aspirations for a bit of sophistication in their lives.

A typical Berni Inn menu:

Starters:
Melon Boat with maraschino cherry or Prawn Cocktail

Main course:
Steak, Gammon Steak or Salmon with chips and peas

Dessert:
Black Forest Gateau or a cheese from the cheese board
Irish Coffee and After Eight Mints

(Later they pioneered chicken-in-the-basket.)

The brothers turned numerous historic pubs into Berni Inns (including the old Llandoger Trow). Expansion was rapid, and in the early 1960s the firm was opening a new restaurant around the country every month, until the chain numbered 147 outlets and had long since outgrown its Bristol origins. By the time it was sold to Grand Metropolitan in 1970, Berni Inn had became the biggest restaurant chain outside the USA and the Berni brothers were multi-millionaires. Aldo, despite his strong Italian accent, always claimed to be a true Bristolian and lived in his bungalow in Clifton with his wife Esme, until he died in 1997. Frank retired to Jersey, where he died in 2000. Grand Met expanded the brand to absorb its own Schooner Inns but the name of Berni was lost when everything was sold to Whitbread and the inns were renamed Beefeater Pubs. Although Berni Inns eventually acquired an image of 'naff', they were the first to bring good-quality, affordable dining-out to the British masses and for many years people couldn't get enough of it.

Suddenly everyone wanted to eat out without being grand. By the late 1960s, the more trendy areas of Bristol had several thriving coffee bars and pubs populated by art and drama students and a motley group of older bohemian types. There was one in particular, a Spanish-style coffee bar in Princess Victoria Street, Clifton, called Number Ten, which first attracted the young Keith Floyd into becoming a pioneering restaurateur and celebrity chef. It had been decorated with classic bullfight posters, Chianti bottles and raffia place mats and, according to Floyd, served 'appalling' omelettes, tinned soups or chilli con carne: 'a horrid concoction of minced meat, roughly chopped tinned tomatoes and tinned kidney beans poured over a mound of minced beef in a saucepan and boiled up with two little cardboard tubes of something like Co-op cayenne pepper'. The drink offered was a 'mind-altering, fight-inducing, foul blend' of Spanish wine called Rocama. Floyd renamed the place Bistro Ten and replaced the menu with French-inspired 'stuffed peppers, sweetbreads in black butter, authentic soupe à l'oignon gratinée, scampi Newburg and all the other semi-French dishes I had learned second-hand over the last couple of years.' Out went the hippy art students and in came a smarter young set with more money and better ideas about food. Floyd, however, told one story of members of the Clifton Club who conned Floyd into serving them free food in his bistro by bringing slugs with them, dropping them into their salad and complaining.

'And so began the carousel of my restaurant career', Floyd wrote in his autobiography *Out of the Frying Pan*. Inspired by the Hole in the Wall restaurant in Bath run by George Perry-Smith, who told Floyd to read Elizabeth David's book on Mediterranean cooking, Floyd was soon juggling three very different kinds of eateries in Bristol. In The Old Granary, a huge, 150-seat restaurant in a jazz club in Bristol Docks, he tried to follow the format of the new and highly successful Berni Inns with steaks, chops and large, steaming bowls of goulash. They were dishes that could be prepared simply and quickly on the grill or in huge pots, ready to be ladled out and 'whizzed off in minutes to the tables by young and enthusiastic waiters and waitresses with no previous skills in the restaurant trade, to hungry, hyped-up customers revelling in the jazz scene'. Floyd recalled it as a joyous and exciting experience, but his passion for cooking and good food went far beyond his ability to run a business – with often disastrous financial results. He later ran other, more successful venues in Bristol, including: Floyd's Bistro in Princess Victoria Street, Clifton; Floyd's Restaurant in Alma Vale Road, with an upmarket menu of fresh-sourced fish, meat and game and fine wines; and Floyd's Chop House in Chandos Road, Redland, an Edwardian-style chop house serving lamb chops with reform sauce, faggots and peas, boiled ham with parsley sauce and game pies, followed by spotted dick and custard and 'a demonic sherry trifle'. Despite three of his restaurants being rated in *The Good Food Guide*, Floyd continued to suffer financial difficulties. He eventually sold the restaurants, plus the rights to his name, and sailed away to new culinary adventures in the South of France, followed by a long and successful career as a television chef.

Bristol diners, their taste buds awakened, were left impoverished by the loss of Floyd and his passion for food adventures. Fortunately, other people

West meets East:
'Indian snacks,
pies and pasties'

of independent vision and passion came to fill the gap, such as Shirley Ann Bell and John Payne, who opened Bell's Diner in 1976 in Montpelier and later bought the Colston Street brewery. As wider travel and books by writers such as Elizabeth David opened people's eyes to the pleasure of the Mediterranean, French, Spanish and Italian-style food began livening up traditional English eating houses with pizzas and spaghetti Bolognese, veal escalope and salad Niçoise with garlic and olive oil. But the real food revolution had already begun in the backwaters of provincial cities across the country with Indian curry and Chinese chop suey.

It is said that many early Indian and Chinese restaurants in Britain were started by sailors jumping ship and finding themselves out of work in one of the big city ports such as Bristol. They took over existing cafés and fish or pie and chip shops and gradually introduced some elements of their home-country cooking. Few of these men would have had much idea how to cook as their mothers and wives traditionally did, or even how to fry a chip or bake a good pasty. Many either married local girls or sent for their womenfolk from home. As they settled into communities, a whole family would work in the restaurant and live above it. Feroze Ahmed, from East Pakistan, founded Bristol's first Indian restaurant in Stoke's Croft and later opened several more, including one on Whiteladies Road which he ran as an English restaurant during the day and as an Indian restaurant called Taj Mahal in the evenings. 'At home, men never cook', he said. 'When we came over, we had to learn to cook for ourselves.'

But they quickly discovered what Englishmen liked to eat. Show an Indian family of any region – Bengali, Gujarati or Punjabi – a menu from an Anglo-Indian restaurant and they will tell you that at home they don't eat or cook the dishes listed. Fierce anglicized curries like the notorious 'vindaloo' – a macho challenge for a generation of lager louts – were totally unlike subtly spiced regional Indian dishes. It was the same story in Chinese restaurants: chop suey and sweet-sour chicken bore no relation to the delicate blend of flavours in Chinese or Thai cooking. Several establishments did, however, cook authentic cuisine for their own people and provided social centres, places to meet friends and offer support in an alien land where their way of life and cooking was regarded with considerable suspicion. But as Anglo-Indian and Anglo-Chinese eateries proliferated around the country, they brought about a change to affordable eating out.

By the 1950s, as the migrant population exploded, many kinds of intriguing new flavours and exotic odours had permeated the city streets, though not everyone found them enticing. As a city port, Bristol has always been a magnet for migrants and absorbed wave after wave of occupiers, settlers and refugees. In medieval Bristol, there had been significant numbers of Welsh and Irish settlers, as well as a small Jewish community. In the sixteenth and seventeenth centuries merchants from France, Spain and Portugal set up businesses in the city and later retired here. After the Reformation, refugees from religious persecution, such as Protestant Huguenots from France and Flemish weavers from the Low Countries, found sanctuary in Bristol. Over time, waves of refugees, displaced people and migrants from around the world arrived in the city looking for a better life. Despite its traditional aversion to foreigners (by which they meant anyone not Bristol-born), Bristol took in large numbers, especially Jews and East Europeans, during and after World War II. After Indian independence in 1959, a hugely diverse range of people from India, Pakistan and Bangladesh came, and later many Asian families thrown out of Uganda made their homes here. Meanwhile, people continued to arrive looking for work from Ireland, Poland, Italy, the Ukraine and the Mediterranean, and during the 1950s and '60s a large community from the Caribbean, in particular Jamaica, became settled in the St Paul's area. Many newcomers to Bristol found employment in the tobacco and sugar businesses and at Fry's chocolate factory, and many women trained as nurses. More recently, the city's workforce has benefitted from a large Polish and Baltic community and found home for refugees from Iraq, Iran and Somalia. They have all brought with them their own values, traditions, religion, culture – and cooking.

But by the 1980s, residents in some areas of the city felt 'swamped' by outsiders. Bristol was described as a 'slumbering volcano', as heavy-handed police and authorities tried to contain the unrest. There was hostility to 'immigrant' lifestyles and 'foreign' cooking: 'You could smell their curries five doors away.' Spices, bright-coloured dishes, pungent odours and alien-looking ingredients aroused disgust but also curiosity: 'I wouldn't know what to do with that,' one housewife said to her friend, looking askance at a breadfruit in the market, 'you don't know where it's been.' It was reminiscent of the fifteenth century, when Bristol citizens responded with a mix of curiosity and fear of new foods like the tomato and potato, only this time it was soya, chilli, Jamaican plantain and callaloo. Fortunately, curiosity was again the winner – but initially on very English terms.

For the people from around the world who have settled in Bristol, however, their traditional food was often the strongest link with home and their past. Food sent from home was especially valued, as Terri Quayne recalled in his memoir, *Taking It on the Road*:

> Ties with 'back home' were kept alive by the yearly exchange organised by my grandfather at Christmas. From the end of the war, we would send a parcel of clothing to his family in the Caribbean and we would get in return the most exciting parcel you could imagine … mangoes, paw-paw, breadfruit, a coconut, sugar cane and black, black Christmas cake dripping with rum … We were home!

SHOPPING

By the mid 1960s, as a number of small self-service stores appeared on high streets, the British had begun their long love affair with convenience shopping. Housewives could serve themselves without the bother of queuing up to have their bacon sliced, cheese portion cut or biscuits weighed. Self-service stores offered a greater choice than small grocery stores; large freezers stocked a tantalising range of ready-prepared frozen foods such as lasagne, chicken korma and gateaux. It was the high-street grocer that paved the way for self-service supermarkets and, in the end, lost out to them. In 1875, a small Bristol family grocer's on Lawrence Hill called J. H. Mills was so successful it expanded to 12 stores and by the 1950s had become a chain called Gateway Foodmarkets (so-named because Bristol was the 'Gateway to the West Country'), later Somerfield's. In 2009, Somerfield's was taken over by the Co-operative Group, which still operates several supermarkets in Bristol. But there was a hidden cost in the convenience shopping trolley.

More and more supermarkets and shopping centres were built, driving out local shops, and the number of traditional food shops continued to fall. The growth in car ownership encouraged people to do a large shop once a week and enormous superstores were built out of town where car parks could be provided. As the number of homes with freezers grew rapidly (two out of five households owned a freezer by 1979), frozen food became more widely eaten; the microwave was another major invention which changed the way we cooked and ate. New products were developed, such as frozen burgers, boil-in-the-bag fish, microwavable ready-made dishes, instant soups and bottled sauces – though not all innovations, such as instant tea, survived the test of time.

If you look now at how most families cook and eat it is not quite the depressing experience that one might have expected. The endless stories in the media: the gloom and finger wagging about obesity; diets with excessive salt, fat and sugar; the cheating and adulteration of our food and the distance we have put between us and where our food comes from – many of these issues have been going on at least since people stopped producing their own food and went to live in the towns. An unhealthy diet, due either to over-indulgence, ignorance or poverty, has been commonplace through history and cheating with weight, content and sourcing was as common in the Middle Ages as it is today. But there are now other pressing global issues to which food production is central.

Mass-produced food may be cheaper and more convenient but it threatened the livelihood of small food producers and retailers such as the corner shop, local markets and specialist food shops on the high street selling cheese, breads, fruit and vegetables, fish and meat. The so-called modern 'food revolution' began to seem a sad indicator of progress; perhaps all we could hope for in the twenty-first century was a diet of bland, ready-made, processed food.

But things have been changing, certainly in Bristol.

BEYOND BAKED BEANS – BRISTOL, CITY OF FOODIES

Despite its long historical association with food, one could not claim that Bristol has always been a Mecca for good food. Nor, as Keith Floyd so graphically observed, had its citizens been especially passionate about the taste and quality of what they ate. But that is all changing and Bristol now proudly bears the informal label 'City of Foodies' – and with good reason.

Suddenly Bristol started bursting with eating places of almost every nationality, with cafes, gastropubs and street-food venues, and, in the more fashionable parts, some top-of-the-range 'celebrity chef' restaurants. The City's love for fine dining has attracted Jamie Oliver, Carluccio and Hugh Fearnley-Whittingstall to open restaurants. But there are plenty of local restaurateurs and chefs who have created their own very individual eateries. After Bell's Diner, Shirley Ann Bell moved on to create the famous riverstation in the old river police station on the harbour front. Barney Haughton came to Bristol to start his first restaurant Rocinantes, in 1988, and went on to open Quartier

Callaloo, sometimes *bhaaji*, is the name used in the Caribbean to refer to different kinds of green leafy plants which are similar to spinach, such as *taro*, *dasheen*, *amaranth* or water spinach. Callaloo is sold in markets in bundles of about six stalks, and the leaves are stripped from the stalks before cooking.

Callaloo

Callaloo is also the name for popular Caribbean dishes which originated in West Africa, created by enslaved Africans who combined African okra with indigenous Caribbean plants. Most countries in the Caribbean have their own versions of dishes made with callaloo, and in some it is the name for a type of soup – Dominica is famous for its Crab and Callaloo Soup. Callaloo is the national dish of Trinidad and Tobago, where it is cooked with okra and coconut milk. In Jamaica, callaloo is traditionally often combined with saltfish – especially cod – and is usually seasoned with tomatoes, onion, escallion (spring onion) and Scotch Bonnet peppers and steamed. It is also popular eaten with roasted breadfruit, boiled green bananas and dumplings as a breakfast dish.

A Recipe for Jamaican Cod and Callaloo
½ lb saltfish (dried, salt cod). You can buy tinned salt cod. It won't need soaking, but will not have as good a texture and flavour.
1 lb fresh callaloo. You can buy tinned callaloo or use English kale or spinach, although they are not quite the same.
3 tbsp olive oil
1 chopped onion, and perhaps some chopped spring onion
½ red, yellow and green peppers
1 tsp chopped or dried thyme
2 crushed garlic cloves
1 Scotch Bonnet pepper, chopped and de-seeded
¼ cup water
1 large tomato, chopped
Black pepper

Soak the saltfish for at least 8 hours, changing the water several times to remove the salt. Simmer the fish for about 20 minutes. Remove from water and allow to cool. Gently flake the fish and remove any bones.

Wash the callaloo and shake dry. Strip the leaves from the stalks. Using a potato peeler or sharp knife, peel the skin from the stalks. Roughly shred the leaves and stalks, but not too fine (about ½-in pieces). Rinse and set aside to drain.

Melt the butter in a frying pan and add the chopped onion, peppers, thyme, garlic and Scotch Bonnet. Cook gently for about 5 minutes. Add the chopped callaloo with the water, cover and steam for 15 minutes. Add the chopped tomato and flaked fish and steam for a further 10 minutes. Remove the lid and reduce any remaining liquid. Season to taste with black pepper.

This recipe is from Beverley Forbes of the Plantation restaurant.

Bristol Sweetmart, St Mark's Road Easton

Vert and then Bordeaux Quay. Many are still flourishing under new management. Harking back to the middle ages and Bristolian love of street food, Tristan Hogg and John Simon came up with the wholly original Pieminister, a pie shop selling a range of pies to suit all tastes. Other innovative pioneers include Papadeli, Tart, Clifton Sausage, Maitreya, the Lido, Olive Shed and Thali Café. New young chefs and passionate restaurateurs with fresh ideas continue to open their doors. Some come and some go and to name just this few is to risk missing others equally as good. But they give a flavour of the sheer breadth and variety of Bristol's eating choices.

Nowadays, almost everyone seems to be talking about food; TV shows, magazines, cookery books, newspapers and websites are awash with recipes, seductive pictures and food celebrities making a fortune from the new food boom. But in Bristol, food is something worth talking about as it is a campaigning movement. Bristolians are taking a fresh interest in cooking and eating and they want to taste food made with care and passion. Moreover, they want to know who made it and where it has come from. Bristol can also boast neighbourhood streets lined with independent food shops, several street markets and farmer's markets selling fresh local produce. More recently there are also night markets, pop-up restaurants and secret supper clubs. The choice is enormous, always changing and seemingly limitless.

Bristol is Britain's capital of the organic movement and home to the headquarters of the Soil Association. The city supports a range of innovative, groundbreaking ideas such as the Slow Food Market, numerous festivals such as Grillstock, Vegfest, Harbourside, the Real Food and Organic Food festivals and the Love Food Spring Festival. There are street-food collectives such as StrEAT and Bristol Eats (BEATS) that combine the best of global street food with music and performance arts. Barny Haughton's real passion has long been concerned with locally sourced, seasonal, sustainable and organic produce, and as well as spreading the word, he went on to run the Square Food Foundation in Knowle, where his cookery school is dedicated to teaching everyone – children and adults – about affordable, nutritious, seasonal, well-sourced and delicious cooking. As he says:

> There is definitely a food revolution taking place: foraging, pop-up restaurants and community farm gardens are all initiatives coming from the people, connecting people back to the land, communities and good food. These initiatives are not driven by profit, they are driven by individuals reclaiming ownership of the food they eat. These are exciting times for food education.

The best food is constantly evolving, fusing and adapting, while still retaining its origins from dozens of different sources – English, Jewish, Indian, Italian, Asian, Spanish, Chinese, Turkish, French, Polish, African Caribbean – and so on. So many ethnic restaurants and food stores reflect a celebration of differences and a respect for and enjoyment of the wonderful culinary traditions brought to Bristol from around the world. They are reminders of all the exotic foods that over the centuries have arrived on Bristol ships.

The best restaurants and food shops in Bristol, whatever their nationality, are community based and rooted in the local economy. Shoppers can buy fish fresh-caught from West Country ports, cheeses from local cheese makers and dairies, vegetables and fruits from neighbouring farms and orchards, lamb from Welsh hills, and meats from nearby farms and local smokeries. There are also plenty of specialist stores selling authentic supplies where anyone can stock up with the vast choice of ingredients and cook their own national dish at home.

Bristol Sweetmart in Easton, east Bristol, was established by the late Kassam Majothi, who, with his family, fled from Uganda to the UK in 1978. An experienced businessman but with limited funds, Mr Majothi started his business as a humble one-shop family business selling Indian sweetmeats and homemade foods. Now this Aladdin's Cave of specialities from around the world is run by the third generation and has grown in strength and size. It has expanded down St Marks Road and attracted other stores and restaurants to join in and create a vibrant street visited by people from across the city. There are many similar stores in Bristol specialising in authentic food ingredients where one can find almost every known variety of spices, oils, pulses, pastas and rice; dried seaweed, bean curd, Chinese ginger and lemongrass, tamarind pods, udon noodles, Spanish pimento, Greek vine leaves, Portuguese salt cod and Jamaican banana leaves; enthusiasts are even growing their own pak choi, okra, chilli and callaloo in their gardens and allotments.

The Gloucester Road is another community-based shopping street famous for its independent multi-cultural stores. Take a walk on a Saturday morning up the Gloucester Road past several traditional top-quality English butchers and as many greengrocers selling locally grown produce, and join the long queue at the famous bakery or buy some fresh fish. Stand and salivate in the Turkish shop displaying traditional breads, cakes and baklavas and watch the woman who sits in a little tent every day rolling out hundreds of *gözleme* – a kind of pancake. Wander into the numerous food stores specialising in oriental ingredients or browse a Spanish, Italian or Greek delicatessen. Buy a takeaway from an Indian café, or eat a delicious homemade cake in an English tearoom and in between explore the numerous food shops, cafés, pubs and restaurants, mostly run by families, from Turkey, Iran, Spain, Indonesia, Morocco, Mexico, South Africa, Ireland…

The Gloucester Road might look like an unexceptional high street in an unexceptional neighbourhood of north Bristol, but it has become famous simply because the majority of the shops, cafés and restaurants are independently run by families who care about what they cook and sell and where their food supplies come from. Their customers appreciate that and, instead of the weekly shop at the supermarket, prefer to wander along the Gloucester Road and fill their baskets with some of the best and freshest food in town.

Bristolians have always been independent-minded, self-determined and keen to do things in their own way. Their biggest successes have started out as small enterprises, bringing good ideas together and nurturing good relations with local suppliers. The best food producers keep tasting, trying ideas and growing a little – but not too much. Traditionally, they fiercely resist commercial power imposed on them; at the opening of a Tesco branch in Stokes Croft, the neighbourhood revolted in the way Bristolians have always done when faced with unwanted or unfair action. It illustrates the independent character of a city that has forged its own identity and is determined to create trends rather than just follow them.

Bristol buzzes with exciting and delicious food ideas. To appreciate the very latest that is going on in Bristol, and to understand where the city has come from visit the food shops, farmers' markets, food stalls and restaurants – and then, at some point, sit down to a dish of cod and callaloo and perhaps reflect on Bristol's long voyage from the past and where it is heading in the future.

BIBLIOGRAPHY

Amey, G. *City under Fire: the Bristol Riots and Aftermath*. Bristol 1979.

Baker, E. *Eileen: Memories of a Working-class Girl in Depression and War*. Bristol 2006.

Barrett, W. *The History and Antiquities of the City of Bristol*. Bristol 1982.

Belsey, J. *The West at War*. Bristol 1990.

Bettey, J.H. *Bristol Observed*. Bristol 1986.

Brown, H.G., and Harris, P.J. *Bristol*. Bristol 1946.

Coles, J., and Minnit, S. *'Industrious and Fairly Civilised': The Glastonbury Lake Village*. Taunton 1995.

Cottle, B. *Joseph Cottle and the Romantics: The Life of a Bristol Publisher*. Bristol 2008.

Dening, C.F.W. *Old Inns of Bristol*. Bristol 1943.

Dresser, M. *Slavery Obscured: The Social History of the Slave Trade*. Bristol 2001.

Dresser, M., and Ollerenshaw, P., eds. *The Making of Modern Bristol*. Bristol 1996.

Dyer, C. *Everyday Life in Medieval England*. London 1994.

Edwards, T. *Bristol*. London 1951.

Eickelmann, C., and Small, D. *Pero: The Life of a Slave in Eighteenth-century Bristol*. Bristol 2004.

Fleming, P. and Costello, K. *Discovering Cabot's Bristol: Life in the Medieval and Tudor Town*. Bristol 1998.

Frank, J., ed. *The Diary of Sarah Fox, née Champion: Bristol 1745-1802*. Bristol 2003.

Frenchay Village Museum. *J.S. Fry & Sons: A Rough Guide to the Family and Firm*. Bristol 2010.

Haddrell, I. *Lockleaze*. Stroud 2010.

Harrison, D., ed. *Bristol between the Wars*. Bristol 1984.

Hibbert, C. *The English: A Social History, 1066-1945*. London 1988.

Hochschild, A. *Bury the Chains*. London 2005.

Horspool, D. *Why Alfred Burned the Cakes*. London 2007.

Hunt, T. *The English Civil War*. London 2002.

Jenks, S. *Robert Sturmy's Commercial Expedition to the Mediterranean*. Bristol 2006.

Latimer, J. *The Annals of Bristol in the Seventeenth Century*. Bristol 1970.

Latimer, J. *The Annals of Bristol in the Eighteenth Century*. Bristol 1970.

Latimer, J. *The Annals of Bristol in the Nineteenth Century*. Bristol 1970.

Little, B. *The City and County of Bristol: A Study in Atlantic Civilisation*. Bristol 1954.

McGrath, P. *Bristol and the Civil War*. Bristol 1981.

MacGrath, P., ed. *Bristol in the Eighteenth Century*. Dorset 1972.

MacInnes, C.M. *A Gateway of Empire*. Bristol 1968.

Marcy, P.T. *Eighteenth-century Views of Bristol and Bristolians*. Bristol 1966.

Marshall, E. *The Two Swords: A Story of Old Bristol*. Bristol 2012.

Maund, V.A. (Pseud.: V.A.M.) *The Diary of a Bristol Woman, 1938-1945*. Bristol 1951.

Morison, S.E. *The European Discovery of America*. Oxford 1971.

Mortimer, I. *The Time Traveller's Guide to Medieval England*. London 2008.

Mortimer, I. *The Time Traveller's Guide to Elizabethan England*. London 2012.

Parsons, C. *The Story of Newfoundland*. Toronto 1949.

Payne, H. *Bristol Riots, 1686-1831*. Bristol 1967.

Pool, A.L. *The Domesday Book to Magna Carta*. Oxford 1964.

Porter, R. *English Society in the Eighteenth Century*. London 1982.

Power, E. *Medieval People*. London 1924.

Priestley, J.B. *English Journey*. London 1934.

Reid, H. *Bristol & Co.: the Story of Bristol's Long-running Businesses*. Bristol 1987.

Reid, H. *Lots of Bottle: An A-Z of Wine*. Bristol 1996.

Reid, H. *On the Waterfront: The Hotwells Story*. Bristol 2002.

Reid, H. *Life in Victorian Bristol*. Bristol 2005.

Richmond, I. *Roman Britain*. London 1963.

Sacks, D.H. *The Widening Gate: Bristol and the Atlantic Economy, 1450–1700*. Bristol 1991.

Shipley, S.P. *Bristol: Siren Nights*. Bristol 1943.

Sisman, A. *Wordsworth and Coleridge: The Friendship*. London 2007.

Tomalin, C. *Samuel Pepys*. London 2002.

Underdown, T.H. *Bristol under the Blitz*. Bristol 1942.

Wall, R. *Bristol, Maritime City*. Bristol 1981.

Williams, N. *The Life and Times of Elizabeth I*. London 1972.

Williamson, J. *The Cabot Voyages and Bristol Discovery under Henry VII*. Bristol 1962.

LOCAL HISTORY PAMPHLETS PRODUCED BY THE BRISTOL BRANCH OF THE HISTORICAL ASSOCIATION

Boore, E. *Excavations at Tower Lane*. Bristol 1984.

Branigan, K. *The Romans in the Bristol Area*. 1969.

Carus-Wilson, E.M. *The Overseas Trade of Bristol in the Later Middle Ages*. 1937.

Carus-Wilson, E.M. *The Merchant Adventurers of Bristol in the Fifteenth Century*. 1962.

Farr, G. *Bristol Shipbuilding in the Nineteenth Century*. 1971.

Fleming, P. *Political History of Bristol Castle*. 2004.

Higgins, D. *The History of the Bristol Region in the Roman Period*. 2005.

Higgins, D. *The Bristol Region in the Sub-Roman and Early Anglo-Saxon Periods*. 2006.

Jones, D. *Bristol's Sugar Trade and Refining Industry*. 1996.

Marshall, P. *The Anti-slave Trade Movement in Bristol*. 1968.

McGrath, P. *Bristol and the Civil War*. 1981.

McGrath, P. *Bristol and America, 1480-1631*. 1997.

Quinn, B. *Sebastian Cabot and Bristol Exploration*. 1993.

Sivier, D. *Anglo-Saxon and Norman Bristol*. 2002.

Thomas, S. *The Bristol Riots*. 1974.

Vanes, J. *The Overseas Trade of Bristol in the Sixteenth Century*. 1975.

Vanes, J. *The Port of Bristol in the Sixteenth Century*. 1977.

Vanes, J. *Bristol at the Time of the Spanish Armada*. 1988.

Waite, V. *The Bristol Hotwells*. 1960.

A SELECTION OF FOOD HISTORY BOOKS

Brears, P. *Food and Cooking in Sixteenth-century Britain*. London 1985.

Brears, P. *Food and Cooking in Seventeenth-century Britain*. London 1985.

Brears, P. *Cooking and Dining in Medieval England*. Devon 2012.

Brears, P., Black, M., Renfrew, J., Stead, J., and Corbishley, G. *A Taste of History: 10,000 Years of Food in Britain*. London 1993.

Coe, S. and M.D. *The True History of Chocolate*. London 1996.

Colquhoun, K. *Taste: The Story of Britain through Its Food*. London 2007.

Davidson, A., ed. *The Oxford Companion to Food*. Oxford 1999.

Dawson, M. *Plenti and Grase: Food and Drink in a Sixteenth-century Household*. London 2009.

Dickson Wright, C. *A History of English Food*. London 2011.

Dorrest, D. *Tea for the British*. London 1973.

Drummond, J.C., and Wilbraham, A. *The Englishman's Food*. London 1939.

Floyd, K. *Out of the Frying Pan: An Autobiography*. London 2000.

Hammond, P. *Food and Feast in Medieval England*. London 2005.

Hardyment, C. *A Slice of Life: The British Way of Eating since 1945*. London 1995.

Hartley, D. *Food in England*. London 1954.

Henisch, B.A. *Fast and Feast: Food in Medieval Society*. London 1976.

Hughes, K. *The Short Life and Long Times of Mrs Beeton*. London 2005.

Mason, L., and Brown, C. *Traditional Foods of Britain: An Inventory*. Devon 1999.

Mason, L., ed. *Food and the Rites of Passage*. Devon 2002.

Minns, R. *Bombers and Mash*. London 1980.

Shephard, S. *Pickled, Potted and Canned: The Story of Food Preserving*. London 2000.

Sim, A. *Food and Feast in Tudor England*. London 1997.

Tager, J. *The Food Chronology*. New York 1995.

Tannahill, R. *Food in History*. London 1973.

Thirsk, J. *Food in Early Modern England*. London 1996.

Wilson, C. Anne. *Food and Drink in Britain*. London 1973.

Wilson, C. Anne, ed. *Waste Not Want Not*. Edinburgh 1989.

Wilson, C. Anne, ed. *'Banquetting Stuffe'*. Edinburgh 1991.

INDEX